ETMEN

An untold story of the H-Block hunger strike

Richard O'Rawe

NEW
ISLAND

Copyright © 2005 Richard O'Rawe

Blanketmen
First published 2005
by New Island
2 Brookside
Dundrum Road
Dublin 14

www.newisland.ie

The author has asserted his moral rights.

isbn 1 904301 67 3

British Library Cataloguing in Publication Data.
A CIP catalogue record for this book is available from the British Library.

Typeset by New Island
Cover design by Fidelma Slattery @ New Island
Printed in Ireland by ColourBooks

10 9 8 7 6 5 4 3 2 1

Go tell the Spartans, thou who passeth by,
That here, obedient to their laws, we lie.

Epitaph for the Spartans who died at Thermopylae
Simonides, c. 556–468 BC;
attributed, Herodotus's Histories

PROLOGUE

It was eight o'clock on the evening of 5 July 1981. Inside the cells in the H-Blocks of Long Kesh Prison were hundreds of IRA prisoners, my friends and comrades, men who had been captured and jailed for their part in our decade-long war to expel the British from the North of Ireland. For over three months some of our number had been on hunger strike to achieve political status, and four comrades had died slow, agonising deaths. I was public-relations officer for the prisoners and Brendan 'Bik' McFarlane was their commander. That night there was a hush of expectation about the wing because Bik had been summoned to a meeting earlier that day in the prison hospital. As a result of that meeting, Bik and I had urgent business to discuss. As usual, this was done in Irish, so that the hated 'screws', the prison warders, wouldn't be able to understand us. I called Bik up to his cell window.

'Well, Rick?' he asked.

'I think there's enough there, Bikso.'

'I agree. I'll write to the outside an' let them know our thinkin'.'

With these words, the leadership of the republican prisoners in the H-Blocks accepted a set of proposals that had been presented to them by the 'Mountain Climber', an intermediary from the British government – four days before the fifth hunger striker, Joe McDonnell, died. Why then did Joe and five other hunger strikers eventually die? In this book, I have attempted to answer that question and to shed some much-needed light on the real story of the hunger strike. In doing so, I believe I have peeled away the layers of carefully scripted myths that have surrounded this momentous event in Irish history, the most insidious being that the prisoners were always in complete control of the hunger strike. As verified by the above conversation, if the prisoners had been free to make the critical decisions, Joe McDonnell and our five comrades who followed him to their graves would be alive today.

Some may ask why I am writing about these things now. Why did it take twenty-four years for me to tell this story? There are several reasons. I was told in 1991, when I privately criticised the role of the IRA Army Council in the hunger strike, that I could be shot for opening my mouth. The threat had the desired effect. As well as that, I was reluctant to expose certain individuals in the leadership of the republican movement to the possibility of criticism, while other IRA Volunteers were giving their lives in the same armed struggle for which my ten dead comrades had died. That armed struggle is over. But, most importantly of all, I cannot, in all conscience, continue to acquiesce in the duplicity that has surrounded the hunger strike from that time. I am convinced that the truth, as I knew it to be, should be told and that I have a duty to the dead hunger strikers to explain fully the events that led to their deaths.

I bear no grudge against the republican movement or any individual in it. In fact, I believe that the movement has been the engine for change in the North and, in my experience, republicans are dedicated people who believe not only in unifying and freeing our country, but also in equality and justice for all – including unionists. I met some of the best people one could encounter in the movement.

I dedicate this book to our ten dead comrades, who gave their lives for the Republic.

1

'Take a good look at it, Rick. If we go ahead with this job, we're not goin' to be seein' it for a long time,' my friend Dollhead said.

Involuntarily, my eyes scrutinised the top of Belfast's Whiterock Road, the tiny commercial heart of the Greater Ballymurphy area. Before me was a threadbare tapestry of nondescript shops, a bar surrounded by a protective cage of grey wire mesh, the ubiquitous Chinese takeaway, and graffiti-covered walls. It was hardly the Champs Élysées – but it was home.

'What makes ya think we'll not be seein' it for a long time?'

''Cause this job's a fuckin' suicide mission! Rick, have ya done a dummy run on it?'

'Nah, I haven't. Jesus Christ, Dollhead, this isn't like you at all. It can't be that bad, surely. Fuck sake, it's just a shitty oul' bank robbery!'

'Shitty oul' bank robbery, my balls! Rick, I swear to God, it is that bad, an' worse. Have ya any idea how far away Mallusk is?'

'Nope, an' I don't care. The job has to be done, an'

that's it. An' we've been told to do it, so we've no choice.'

'Well, wait till I tell ya something: I'm not doin' it. No fuckin' way. Mark these words, Rick: if we rob this bank, we'll not be back here for a long time – if we come back at all. I'll resign from the 'RA before I'll do this bank.'

'Hell's bells, I've never seen ya like this.'

'Do a dummy run, Rick. Just do it,' Dollhead said, and walked away up Dermotthill.

I watched him until he disappeared around the bend at the bottom of the Dermotthill Estate, wondering all the while why he was so spooked by the prospect of robbing this bank – an operation which, relatively speaking, was on the lower rungs of IRA activity.

I went over and sat on the concrete surround of the grass verge at the bottom of the estate. All around me people were going about their daily business, unaware that I was observing them. Kevin 'Whack' McGettigan and Paddy 'The Prod' McMullan were pressing the buzzer on the steel door at the side of Kelly's bar in the hope of gaining entry to get 'the cure'; the two lads looked like they needed it. I noticed wee Lily Hall coming out of McAulfield's butchers and then walking the short distance to McAvoy's grocery shop, while Geordie Finn was going into the post office to collect his customers' dole money. (Geordie would collect people's dole and deliver it to their houses for a small fee.)

It was on occasions like this that I envied the much-maligned residents of Ballymurphy: I was jealous of their routine lives and their ability to confront the misfortune of having been born the unwanted children of a state that viewed them as whinging malcontents and rebels. Not one of them had to deal with the dangers of robbing a bank in two days' time, or sweat a comrade's sixth sense, which screamed at him that to go ahead with this robbery meant either imprisonment or death. Sometimes, when I sat back and looked at the way my life was panning out, I regretted having inherited my father's passion for rebellion and revolution, for forcing the British to leave Ireland through armed struggle. (This passion was the reason I had joined the Provisional IRA at the age of seventeen in March 1971.) But those regrets were always suppressed by my desire to end British rule in the North of Ireland and to establish a thirty-two-county socialist Republic.

As I watched people go about their business, my mind turned once again to the coming bank robbery. There was a job to be done, and no amount of hocus-pocus would alter that fact: I had to put Dollhead's mystic reticence to bed. There was no room for negative thinking: an operation was an operation, even if it was only a 'shitty oul' bank robbery'. And, besides, this was my opportunity to make amends for an earlier *faux pas*.

On that occasion, another volunteer and I had gotten drunk in Kelly's bar, and when we ran out of money we decided to do a 'homer', which is an IRA euphemism for a self-gain robbery. We borrowed a sympathiser's vehicle, one that most Volunteers in our Battalion knew to have been used regularly by the Ballymurphy Volunteers, and drove down the Falls Road. We robbed the first place that caught our eye. We were unmasked while doing the robbery and, while the RUC was not informed of the robbery, the IRA was. Within a couple of hours it had traced the vehicle and identified us (unbeknown to us). We got less than fifty pounds from the robbery and we blew it on drink that night. It was the dearest drink I've ever had in my life.

We were both shot for our misdemeanour, and rightly so. Drunk or not, we had brought the IRA into disrepute. Although we were only meant to be grazed in one leg, the bullet had gone straight through my right leg and had hit a bone on my left leg. My friend suffered an even worse fate: the bullet shattered his right leg, leaving him with a permanent limp. (Another friend, who was shot along with us, was only grazed.) Fortunately, the IRA had phoned for an ambulance before we were shot and we were quickly transported to the Royal Victoria Hospital.

I had been married only a week when I had been shot (the IRA had delayed my punishment until after my wedding). In fact, I was shot within two hours of returning from my honeymoon in Dublin. My wife, Bernie, was just eighteen years old, but her years belied her wisdom. She kept saying that we would get through this and that we would come out stronger on the other side. She never once asked me why I would do such a silly thing when I was on the threshold of pledging myself to her for the rest of my life.

Months later though, she confessed that I had 'badly hurt' her. Surprisingly, this was not because I had done the homer – she had put that down to a drunken escapade. It was because when she and my father had come into the hospital ward, I had asked her to wait outside while I poured my heart out to him. I didn't realise it at the time, but I had been extremely thoughtless – I had inadvertently devalued her and given her the impression that she did not matter, that my father's feelings were more important than hers. My father had been a life-long republican. Because of my overwhelming need to beg his forgiveness, I had completely ignored the possibility that it must have been a terrible ordeal for Bernie to have to see her husband of one week lying in a hospital bed, having been shot and disgraced by his own organisation.

When my father came into the ward later that day, I cried a bucketful of tears: I will never forget the pained look on his face. I couldn't apologise enough to him, knowing that I had betrayed him as a son and had let down the family – let alone the great dishonour I had brought on myself. He saw that I was hurting and tried to comfort me by saying that life was about learning from, and living with, mistakes, that anyone could make a mistake, and that I wasn't the first and wouldn't be the last to mess up. He hugged me and told me not to worry, that this pain would pass. I so much wanted to hear those words, even though they failed to lessen my feelings of self-detestation or assuage my guilt at having brought shame on my family. I hated myself.

I was released from hospital after a week and refused to leave the house for a couple of weeks. How could I face those good people who had put their trust in me down through the years? A couple of Volunteers called to the house in a car and insisted that I go with them to Kelly's bar for a drink. I reluctantly agreed. When we got there, I was treated very well by everyone and, after a few beers, I felt at home again as the formal greetings gave way to a bout of serious ribbing about my having been shot. It was as well that I was thick-skinned.

I had one abiding objective, one avenue left along which I could salvage my honour and self-respect, and that was to get back into the IRA as quickly as possible. I had found life outside the IRA difficult to adjust to: all my friends and comrades were still in it, and I felt a certain jealousy when I saw them discussing IRA matters to which I was no longer privy. Although I was ideologically committed to the cause, for me, in many ways, being in the IRA was almost the objective rather than the means. I missed the sense of belonging, the comradeship, even the conspiratorial nature of the IRA's procedures. I was still a very committed republican: the struggle had been my life, and I dearly wanted, if the IRA would take me back, to be given the opportunity to atone for my mistake.

After three months, I approached the man who had engineered my punishment and told him that I wanted to be readmitted to the fold. He laughed and told me that there would be no problem. I was back where I belonged.

Two days after our conversation, I met Dollhead early in the morning at the top of the Whiterock Road. It was February 1977, dark and cold, and it was bank-robbery day. There was a wry smile on his face.

'There it is, Rick,' he said. 'The top of the 'Rock. You're not goin' to see it for a long time.'

'Wise up. You're puttin' the scud on us, an' we haven't even started yet.'

'We're goin' down for this one, Rick.'

I wasn't in the least surprised to find Dollhead ready and willing to do a job that frightened the life out of him. He was always going to do this operation, no matter what he had said earlier; his sense of duty to the IRA allowed for nothing else.

We climbed into the white van. There were four of us in the van, all experienced men who had faced this type of pressure many times before. It had been decided that we wouldn't wear gloves until we'd left the van to rob the bank, in case the police – or 'Peelers', as they were more commonly known – stopped us on the way. I was sitting in the front alongside Dollhead, our driver, and made a point of touching nothing. The weapons were in another vehicle, behind us, so that if we were stopped, at least we'd be clean – although, considering the calibre and history of the men in the van, we would be arrested and taken to Castlereagh Interrogation Centre at the very least.

We crossed over to north Belfast. We drove up the never-ending Antrim Road, past the urban New Lodge and the North Circular Road area with its grand detached houses; soon Bellevue Zoo was behind us. I looked quizzically at Dollhead, but he only shook his head and grunted: 'I told ya, didn't I?' I had no reply, but Willie John McAllister wasn't so taciturn.

'In the name of Jesus, where's this bank?' he asked.

'Willie John, we're nowhere near it,' Dollhead said.

'For fuck's sake, if we go any farther away from Belfast, we'll end up in Ballycastle. We must have passed a dozen banks already to get here. Look, there's another one.'

Finally, we came to a halt outside Glengormley village. A female Volunteer left the second vehicle and got into our van. She produced the guns, surgical gloves and pillowcase – the bank robber's tools. After putting on the gloves, we stuck the guns down the backs of our trousers and drove on. We arrived outside the Northern Bank at Mallusk at 11 o'clock. I had never heard of Mallusk before this operation had been proposed, and had no idea where we were. All I knew was that we were miles from the safety of Ballymurphy.

We left the van as any workers would, laughing and patting each other on the back, but that was all for show. Behind the smiles and merriment was the tension that comes when an operation is about to take place.

Everybody had been allocated a job. Willie John was to scoop the money. Another man was to help me to frighten the staff into obeying our orders. I had overall charge of the robbery in the bank, as well as covering the door. Dollhead would remain outside in the van, along with the female Volunteer.

When we entered the bank, Willie John went up to the top of the customers' area and the second man pretended to fill in a form in the middle of the bank. They both gave me the nod that they were ready. I put my hand around the back of my waistband and produced the gun.

'Nobody move! This is a robbery! Get away from that counter or I'll fuckin' blow your heads off!' I shouted as loudly as I could, pointing the gun menacingly at the bank staff.

While the second man ordered all the customers to lie down on the floor, Willie John had a gun pointed at a bank employee and was ordering him to open a door leading into the back of the bank.

The side door was opened and Willie John was in behind the counter in a flash, scooping money from the various teller slots. He then disappeared into the farther reaches of the bank, where I assumed the safe was located.

There is always a period in a bank robbery when the initial threat of violence gives way to the business at hand, as staff and robbers alike resign themselves to getting the ordeal over with as quickly as possible. I was standing at the side of the front door, and although I kept barking orders to ensure control over the staff and customers, I felt very calm and was pleased that things were progressing nicely. An old lady, who was standing at the first teller slot, was in a bit of distress, so I went over to her and told her she had nothing to worry about, that we were only interested in the money and that she was in no danger. She said, 'Thank you, son,' and seemed more settled. A large man entered the bank and I put the gun to his head and shouted at him to put his arms up before making him stretch out on the floor. I then frisked him to see if he was carrying a weapon.

The whole thing was taking too long and I shouted for the 'number three' (Willie John) to hurry up. For the duration of the robbery, I had my hand covering my mouth and face so that, even if there was a hidden camera – and I couldn't see one – at least they would not get a clear image of me.

Finally, Willie John emerged from behind the counter. One last warning that nobody should move, and we were out of the bank. We walked quickly to the van and jumped in. As the van took off, the guns and gloves were put into the pillowcase, along with the money, and the pillowcase was then shoved into a two-wheeled shopping trolley. We settled down then, although it was hard to 'act normal' after such an adrenalin rush.

We had barely moved two hundred yards from the bank when Dollhead alerted us to a white car behind us. He speeded up and the white car did the same. The next thing I noticed was a figure hanging out the window with a gun in his hand.

'They're fuckin' Peelers! There's a fucker pointin' a gun at us!' I shouted.

'Shut the fuck up, Rick! I'm tryin' to drive here!'

My stomach was turning: this was the worst of all the many predicaments I had been in. Dollhead somehow put a bit of distance between them and us. As we entered Glengormley village, we dropped off the female Volunteer; she disappeared with the shopping trolley containing the money and the guns. The Peelers came around the corner as we gathered speed, and the chase was on again. We then crashed the lights at Glengormley and sped back up the Antrim Road. The cops followed suit.

By this time, we knew there would be a dozen cop cars zeroing in on us. The two Peelers following us would be on the radio to tell their colleagues where we were, and sooner or later they would throw up a roadblock. We needed to get off the main roads and try to make our escape in the side streets. When a Brit jeep drove in behind the Peelers, our semblance of composure evaporated. At one corner, two of the van's wheels lifted off the road, and the van almost keeled over. We had to throw our weight to the other side of the van to get it back down again.

Eventually, we made our way into a housing estate and the van veered out of control into a garden and crashed. Our last words to each other were to separate, to make it harder for the Peelers to chase us.

I knew that to stay on the street meant capture, so I ran up an alley. There were tall hedges at the back of the alley and a ten-foot drop on the other side. Standing on a concrete bollard, I dived over the hedge, landing and rolling on the other side.

I heard shots and guessed that the Peelers had opened up on one of the lads, but there was little time to think about that. My main objective was to get as far from the crashed van as possible. I ran over to the side of the houses that led to the next street and jerked my head out to see if the coast was clear. I saw Dollhead standing with his hands up, surrounded by cops. At that moment I heard voices coming from the back of the hedges over which I had just vaulted. Two heads peered over the hedge. I stood silent, in full view of the Peelers. I didn't even glance in their direction. (I'd read somewhere that people sensed when they were being watched.) They looked around for a minute and I heard one say: 'He must be farther up the lane.'

When they disappeared, I walked across the road and entered the backs of the houses in the next street. In one garden there was a shed; I stayed in there for a couple of minutes before deciding that sooner or later they would get around to searching the gardens and any sheds or huts that were in them. I moved from street to street, staying in the back gardens all the time and standing still when I heard the whizz of jeeps or the brakes of cop cars.

I was wearing a parka jacket and decided it would be best to ditch it. By that stage, they would have a description of the bank robbers and would be looking for a man in a parka. Anyway, it was too suspicious a garment to be wearing. In a back garden, some way from the crash site, an old man was standing looking at his flower-bed. Without saying a word, I handed the jacket to him. He looked astonished, but nodded his appreciation, and I left.

By now I was well away from the van. I was still in danger, but at least the cops had no idea where I was. Neither had I, though! I cursed the fact that we had given over the guns in Glengormley; if we hadn't, I would have walked into the nearest house with a parked car outside and forced the owner to drive me to Belfast city centre.

I decided that my best course of action was to try and hide out somewhere. There was a school in front of me, and I reckoned it must be in a loyalist district, since I had never heard of any Catholic areas this far out of Belfast. I opened the door of the boiler room and walked in. I was no sooner in the room than the janitor entered and asked me what I was doing. I had to think quickly. I told him I was in the Ulster Volunteer Force and that the cops were after me. I asked him if he could hide me for a couple of hours. He refused to help me and told me to clear off. So it was back on the run, this time across a nearby golf course.

I knew that if I was to escape from this mess, I would have to get transport of some sort into the city centre, but I had no money. We had just emptied a bank of what I later found out to be eleven thousand pounds and I hadn't a brass farthing! Two golfers were teeing off and I asked them for some money, making up a story that I needed to get to the hospital because my pregnant wife had just been taken off in an ambulance. It was ridiculous, but it was the best I could do at the time. They gave me two pounds. I hadn't a clue where I was, but I decided to try and reach the clubhouse and phone a taxi to take me in to Belfast.

The golf course was split in two by a little lane and I lay behind a hedge at the side of the lane as a cop car sped past. The time had come to cross the lane and I ran to the other side of it, only to be nearly knocked down by a second cop car. I ran on over to the other half of the golf course, but I knew the jig was up.

I dived into some undergrowth, desperately trying to think of my next move. The Peelers were already on the course and I was sure that they would have shot me in the back if I had tried to make a run for it. They screamed at me to come out with my hands in the air. I did. After they had frisked me, they used the butts of their machine guns to batter me. It was 'cover-up time' as I put my hands over my face and kept my legs close together to protect my testicles.

More Peelers arrived, possibly twenty of them, and they hammered into me with fervour. They were pulling each other back to get at me. One guy hoisted me to my feet and put his Sterling sub-machine-gun under my chin, threatening to blow my head off. His face was the deepest red, like a huge pimple that was ready to explode, and the venom in his voice left me in no doubt that he meant what he said. He was shrieking that I had shot one of his mates. I hadn't a clue what he was talking about: our guns had been dropped at Glengormley with the female Volunteer, so we couldn't have shot anyone. Just when I thought he was going to finish me off, a sergeant arrived. He pulled 'Tomato Face' off me and punched me a few times himself. Then I was put into a cop car and driven to Newtownabbey Police Station.

On the way there, Dollhead's words rang in my ears: 'Take a good look at it, Rick. If we go ahead with this job, we're not goin' to be seein' it for a long time.'

Why hadn't I listened to my friend? My mind was doing somersaults. What would Bernie say when she found out what had happened? We had been married only six months and she believed I was no longer an IRA Volunteer. Now she was going to find out the hard way that I had been lying to her. How would she react? Worse still, it appeared that I had been caught almost red-handed, so she would have to look at the probability of adjusting to my being in prison for a long time. I consciously put her out of my head because I had to deal with the present – which probably meant yet another tanking in the cop shop. At that moment, I wished I was going into Kelly's bar for the cure.

A journey was beginning – a terrible journey that would see me plunge into unimaginable depths of despair.

2

As I looked up in agony at the ceiling from the floor of the holding cell, believing that years in prison awaited me, I felt desolate. Gone was the bravado of the 'RTP' (rough, tough Provie), and in its place was the sobriety of the damned. I was a mess.

I eventually managed to pull myself together, and my brain began to stir again as I attempted to compose a story that would explain why I had been hiding from the Peelers. The problem was I didn't even know where I had been lifted. I decided that I had no choice but to say nothing and reply to every question with: 'I'll answer that when I see my solicitor.'

The door opened and a Peeler came in. His coat was unbuttoned and he was unshaven: with his ginger stubble and thick brown glasses, he looked almost as rough as me. He laughed as he towered over me.

'Boys a boys!' he said. 'Every dog has its day, doesn't it, O'Rawe? I never thought I'd see ya again, an' now you're lyin' like a piece of shit on the floor of my police station.' He walked around me. I didn't take him under my notice.

'Don't ya remember me, Ricky lad?' I knew who he was, right enough. ''Course ya do! We met in another case a few years ago. Ya made a cunt out of me in the witness box, didn't ya? You're not so big now, are ya, ya fuckin' scumbag! You'll not be walkin' this time, ya bastard.'

The Peeler had been one of the detectives who had interviewed me when I had been arrested in 1974 and charged with conspiring to murder a west Belfast man. Despite my dire predicament, I was struck by the irony of our paths crossing again under these circumstances. The wheel had come full circle for him, because he now had the pleasure of seeing his former adversary lying on the floor of his cop shop, defenceless, apparently caught red-handed robbing a bank. I would have taken odds that he skipped the light fandango when he heard my name, but he hadn't been dancing in the High Court in 1974.

The IRA picked up a suspected informer in Kelly's bar at the top of the Whiterock Road in September 1974. He suffered two days of intensive interrogation, during which he had been ill-treated.

Two nights later, detectives hit our house and arrested me for allegedly being involved in the interrogation. I was taken to Springfield Road Police Station, where I denied all knowledge of the affair during the police interviews and gave a cast-iron alibi that put me at work at the time. The cop in Newtownabbey had been one of my interviewers and had made a written statement incorporating my alibi.

Even as I lay on the floor of the cop shop after the bank robbery, I found myself beginning to snigger as some of the funnier memories of the affair returned.

While in the Springfield Road police cells, I had to leave the cell to eat my dinner on a radiator in the corridor. Opposite me, at the other radiator, was a man whom I knew to be Hughie McKee. Hughie wasn't an IRA Volunteer, and I was wondering what he was doing there. A cop must have been reading my mind: he asked Hughie what he was in for.

'Speak up. I can't hear ya,' said Hughie.

'What are ya in for, boy?'

'Boy? Did I hear you callin' me a boy? Do I look like a boy?' (Hughie was about fifty years old, with heavy jam-jar glasses and a Teddy-boy haircut.)

'Okay, well, Mister McKee, what are ya in for?'

'You fuckin' tell me, mister. Some bastard says I beat him up. But I'll tell ya somethin' for nothing: when I get outta here, I fuckin' will beat him up.'

Beating somebody up? Hughie was in for a murder-related charge and I doubted that he was going to have the opportunity to beat anyone up for quite a while.

I was in the process of swallowing some chips when I heard Hughie's outburst, and I nearly choked with laughter at his reply. The Peeler saw my reaction and turned away, reaching for a handkerchief to wipe his eyes. To make matters worse, Hughie indignantly pushed his glasses back on his nose and, seeing the Peeler and me buckled over with laughter, asked: 'Here, what's so fuckin' funny?' Two more Peelers entered the little hallway and asked their colleague what was so amusing, but he couldn't get a word out.

I was charged with conspiracy to murder and sent to Crumlin Road Jail. It was an IRA order that Volunteers did not recognise British courts. Dismissing your legal representation and refusing to recognise the jurisdiction of the court was tantamount to admitting that you were an IRA Volunteer and that in all probability you were guilty, because only IRA men took this course of action. As a result of the order, I dismissed my barrister,

Desmond Boal, QC, when the trial began and set about putting up my own defence. Boal was a former assistant to the Attorney General of Northern Ireland, but he resigned from the Unionist Party to help form the Reverend Ian Paisley's Democratic Unionist Party. No matter about his politics, I detected the scent of an anti-establishment rebel in the character of Mr Desmond Boal. In fact, he had given me invaluable advice which steered me on a course that eventually led to my acquittal.

The only substantive evidence against me was the complainant's assertion that he recognised my voice during one of his interrogations. During a four-hour session with him in the witness box, I tore his evidence asunder.

In conjunction with this, I asked the police inspector in charge of the case if justice would be served by ignoring documented time-sheets from the building site in West Belfast where I worked and material witnesses, both of which put me at work during the time I had allegedly questioned the suspected informer. That forced the judge to intervene and call Patrick Marrinan, my solicitor, to the stand. Mr Marrinan produced time-sheets from the building site where I had been working. These time-sheets bore my signature and verified that I had clocked in that morning for work and clocked out again that night. In the course of their dialogue, Mr Marrinan told the judge that besides the time-sheets, there was other evidence, namely witnesses, who, if called upon, would confirm that I had been working with them and that I hadn't left the site that day.

The cop who had walked into the holding cell in Newtownabbey Police Station after the bank robbery then got into the witness box. He appeared to forget that I had given him an alibi, even though his own written statement verified my alibi claim. I walked free from the court. But for every dry season there is a wet season, and the Peeler was having the last laugh now.

I was driven from Newtownabbey to Castlereagh Police Station, the main interrogation centre in the North. The interviews went as I suspected, with question after question followed by me saying: 'I'll answer that when I see my solicitor.' There was no attempt to beat me up.

Besides requesting the name of the one Volunteer who had escaped the dragnet from the van, the detectives continually pressed me on the name of the female Volunteer. I found that puzzling: how did they know that a female had been with us? She hadn't been in the bank, and they hadn't seen her getting out of the van. Therefore, on the face of it, it appeared that someone was saying more than they should have been. I eventually found out that none of us bank robbers had told them about her. The man with whom the female Volunteer had left the shopping trolley containing the money and guns after she had got out of the white van hadn't been informed about the bank robbery. On seeing the guns and money, he decided to dump the shopping trolley and its contents in an elderly neighbour's house. The son of the elderly neighbour was an Ulster Defence Regiment soldier: when he discovered the shopping trolley, he informed the police. The man with whom the trolley had originally been left was arrested. During police interviews, he confirmed that a girl had been involved, although he didn't identify her – despite the fact that he knew her – or the man who had approached him in the first place for the use of his house.

What perplexed me most was how the white cop car

had been waiting for us when we had come out of the bank. I told myself that maybe it was just a coincidence, an extraordinarily lucky break for them. On the other hand, an informer in the IRA may have tipped off Special Branch.

During one of the interviews, I could hear shouting, thuds and cries of pain from somewhere along the corridor. A detective told me that a couple of the Shankill Butchers were getting the treatment, and they were ratting on each other to minimise their own involvement. (The Shankill Butchers were a band of loyalist killers who had systematically cut the throats of any Catholic unfortunate enough to cross their paths. The Peelers weren't sparing the rod on them, anyway.)

After two days, we were charged with the armed robbery of the Northern Bank at Mallusk. Mallusk. The very name almost made me physically sick. My first words to Dollhead were: 'I'll never doubt you again,' to which he replied: 'Too late, Rick, too late.'

After the obligatory meetings with the governor and prison doctor in Crumlin Road Jail, I was sent to the Royal Victoria Hospital on the Falls Road because the doctor suspected that I had a couple of broken ribs. If I had felt slightly envious of the routine lives of ordinary Ballymurphy people when I had sat at the grass verge at the top of the Whiterock Road, two days before the bank robbery, I now found that morsel of envy turn into a feast of jealousy as I looked out the window of the police Land Rover that was transporting me to the hospital and saw people going about their daily business. But it had been my choice to join the IRA, and I had been fully aware of the consequences of that decision.

I looked for an opportunity to escape, but the cuffs

were never taken off me – even in the X-ray room. The X-rays showed that I had severe internal bruising but that none of my ribs were broken. We returned to the 'Crum'.

3

Crumlin Road Jail was certainly a changed place from when I had last been there in 1974. The British plan to criminalise the struggle was in full throttle; an integral part of their policy was to reject our claim that we were political prisoners by removing the political status that we had won through a hunger strike in 1972. As a result, we were denied segregation and forced to share wings with loyalists. Before we arrived in the jail, there had been scuffles and fighting between both sets of prisoners, but eventually the republican staff and their loyalist counterparts had agreed a system of mutual co-operation: the loyalists would have use of the canteen and yard one day, and we would have them the next. The group not using the facilities would remain locked up all day.

The screws also had a different attitude. They were cockier and cheekier than before, and they made sure we knew that they were in control and that the days of political status were history.

Bernie came up to visit me with our newborn daughter, Bernadette. Bernie had assumed that I had finished with the IRA, and the shock of my arrest must have been shattering for her. She searched my face for answers where none existed. I have to admit that I cried sorely when I saw Bernie with our little baby, and her so distressed at our plight. But she soon rallied and put on a brave face. It was all show, I knew, but it helped to lift the heavy burden of guilt from my shoulders.

Some of the first-timers even fell for the 'Confession' trick, a notorious ploy whereby the victim would be told that it was obligatory for all newcomers to go to Confession. Of course, the 'priest' would be a fellow inmate, and he would attempt to elicit some details of the victim's sex life. It had happened to me in 1973 when I was in Cage 3.

I had known about the Confession routine because this had been my second time interned and we had used it extensively when I was on the prison ship *Maidstone* in 1972. When I first arrived in Cage 3, I was told that I had to go to the drying-hut to have my Confession heard. Joe McDonnell and I (Joe had also been on the *Maidstone*) had a brief talk; afterwards, I made my way to the drying-hut where the 'Confession' would be heard. A curtain with two holes in it separated the 'priest' from the penitent. After I had confessed a few innocuous sins, the priest asked me if I'd anything else to confess.

'Not that I can think of, Father.'

'Have ya ever committed acts of impurity, my son?'

'I had sex with a girl before I was lifted, Father.'

'How many times, my son?'

'Quite a lot, Father.'

'That's all right. Tell me, have ya ever engaged in acts of impurity with yourself?'

'Yes, Father.'

'How many times, my son?'

'This is a bit embarrassin'.'

'Take your time.'

'Well, I've engaged in acts of impurity dozens of times with myself, Father.'

'Dozens of times? How many dozen?'

'I'm not sure, but dozens an' dozens of times.'

'Dozens an' dozens of times? Jesus Christ, you're a prolific wanker, aren't ya, son?'

'Father, I'm sorry.'

'It's all right, my son. God has a big heart. Tell me, what did ya call the girl ya had sex with?'

'I don't like to mention names, Father.'

'God already knows her name. Now what do ya call her?'

The trap had been set: I proceeded to tell him that the girl was his daughter, his daughter's name coming courtesy of McDonnell!

'Ya dirty bastard!' he shouted, and a big boxing glove exploded in my face.

This tomfoolery broke up the monotony in prison. It was incredible, given the well-publicised history of the Confession routine, that people were still falling for it in the Crum in 1977.

In response to the new British criminalisation plan, Kieran 'Header' Nugent, the first republican prisoner to be sentenced after 1 March 1976, started the 'blanket' protest in the newly built H-Blocks of Long Kesh, or the Maze Prison, as the authorities now called it. The 'blanket' protest got its name because Nugent refused to wear the prison regulation clothing (or 'monkey suit', as it was more commonly known) and the screws gave him a blanket to wear instead and locked him in his cell for twenty-four hours a day.

With the last piece in the new British counter-insurgency policy in place, all the authorities had to do was break Nugent and the other protesting prisoners in Long Kesh, along with my friend Jimmy Duffy and our comrades in the basement of the Crum. If they succeeded in overcoming the prisoners' resistance to the new regime and forced them to conform to prison rules, then the British policy-makers believed that the political base for the struggle would evaporate and the IRA could be portrayed as a criminal organisation, rather than a freedom movement. The other essential ingredients in their master plan were the conveyor-belt system of Castlereagh Interrogation Centre, where prisoners were beaten into signing confessions, and the no-jury Diplock courts, which invariably were satisfied to rely on those confessions, despite misgivings being raised in many of the trials. The result of this intricate strategy was that the role of the British army could be dramatically reduced and local forces, principally the Royal Ulster Constabulary and the Ulster Defence Regiment, could deal with the 'criminal' conspiracy. This localisation of the struggle was known as 'Ulsterisation'.

The new Secretary of State for Northern Ireland, Roy Mason, a pygmy of a man, pushed through the criminalisation policy. He talked of 'squeezing the IRA like toothpaste' – and with some justification. The British conveyor-belt system did seem to be working, and it was going to take something extraordinary from the IRA to break the stranglehold.

I applied for bail and, to my surprise, there wasn't much evidence against me. There were no witnesses from the bank, no fingerprints, no confession and very little else. The one damning piece of evidence was the statement of a cop who claimed that he had chased me from the second I had left the van until I had been arrested.

Another Peeler claimed that I had made a verbal admission when I remarked to Dollhead and Willie John, as we were awaiting transport to Townhall Street Police Station to be formally charged, that we were 'gentlemen robbers'. I remembered saying this, but it had been a joke. Anyway, the Peelers didn't think it funny and used this off-the-cuff remark to support their case. My barrister said that if I could prove that I had disappeared from my would-be pursuer's view for even a second, then I would likely be acquitted and my remark would be put down to what it was: a joke.

Time passes slowly in the Crum. 'Bootser' Hughes, Dollhead and myself shared a cell. On the landing above us were loyalists. They seemed a decent bunch. On parcel days, we would send them up some of our meat on a line from the cell window, and they reciprocated on their parcel days. Our conversation was always confined to small talk, but it was friendly enough all the same. Later on, we found out that two of them were members of the Shankill Butchers gang and realised how careless we had been.

Our trial began in February 1978. By this time, IRA Volunteers were allowed to recognise the courts, and I had a barrister representing me. Mr Marrinan was once again my solicitor. He made it crystal clear that, in his assessment, the judge wasn't in the least disposed to doubting the evidence of the Peelers and in all likelihood I would be found guilty. The cops had caught me once upon the hip and wanted their pound of flesh, as Shylock said to Antonio in *The Merchant of Venice*.

A cop went into the witness box. My barrister asked him what had happened to my parka jacket that the people in the bank had said I was wearing. He said that I had thrown it away.

The barrister asked the witness how he could be certain that there wasn't any money or guns in the jacket. The witness said that he had not considered that possibility. I was euphoric with his answer – it was so patently ridiculous that, in my opinion, it negated his entire testimony (like all defendants, I always looked for the blue skies of hope and tried to black out the grey skies of reality). The barrister pursued the line of questioning by asking the witness if any of his superiors had ordered him to try and retrieve the jacket after the search for the bank robbers had been concluded. The witness meekly replied that they had not. What was obvious to me (not being an expert of course) was that if this witness had been chasing me, and if, as he had told the court, I had not left his sight for a second, then he must have seen me discarding the jacket and knew where it was – yet he did not go back to retrieve this important piece of evidence that could have contained money or guns. It did not get much better, as far as I was concerned. The barrister then asked the witness if he expected the court to believe this. The witness mumbled that he was telling the truth.

The old man to whom I had given the coat hadn't turned it over to the Peelers, and it was getting to be a thorn in their side. The cross-examination concluded after my barrister made some more embarrassing points.

But while I had hoped against hope that I would beat the charge, I had more than a suspicion that, no matter how degraded the prosecution case was, I was going down. If the legendary Perry Mason and Rumpole of the Bailey had been defending me, it would not have made any difference.

The judge accepted the prosecution case over mine. Ricardo was going down.

I got eight years. Willie John was sentenced to nine because he had had a previous conviction, and Dollhead got ten years because he had two previous convictions.

We were ecstatic about the 'short' sentences, since some people were getting twenty years for armed robbery. As we made our way back to the Crum through the underground tunnel, a smiling Willie John called our jail terms 'wee buns'. But I knew that the wee buns were going to grow into big buns as the blanket protest opened its arms and welcomed us into its embrace.

4

The reception area in Long Kesh was a hive of activity. Screws and orderlies were busy taking names, allocating us little cubicles and sorting out prison uniforms. I knew some of the screws from the days of internment. One handed me the prison uniform and told me to put it on. I told him that there was no chance of me wearing his outfit. He simply shrugged and muttered: 'Another streaker.'

The darkness of the night dropped like a guillotine as we were transported in a prison van up to H-Block 3. There was a silence in the van as each man looked into the eyes of adversity. It wasn't the miles of razor wire or the thousands of yellow luminescent lights that had made me silent, but rather a premonition that disaster awaited. Something told me that this was going to be the most harrowing voyage of my life. My analysis of the impending situation left no room for happy endings. I found myself slipping into a 'big D' (jail parlance for 'depression') at the thought of it. As we left the minibus, my last thought before entering the block was: 'Ricardo, brace yourself.'

The newly built blocks in Long Kesh were shaped like the letter 'H'. The cross in the middle of the 'H' was known, paradoxically, as 'the circle'. This was where the administration had their offices. Prisoners were kept in the two vertical sides of the 'H'; each side contained two wings. Each wing had twenty-six cells, twenty-five of which were for individual prisoners, with one double cell, Cell 26. Because of the numbers of prisoners going on protest, the prison authorities doubled everyone up and used Cell 26 as a control-and-search location.

Dollhead and myself were put into a cell in C-wing until we could be moved to a functioning protest wing. Gerry 'Blute' McDonnell was in the cell next to us. I had known Blute from internment and from remand. He was a thinking man, someone who was always up for a discussion: we debated the general situation from our cell windows.

Blute was one of those indefatigable characters, the 'don't let the bastards grind you down' type who lived and breathed the IRA. His view was that, eventually, we would break the British government and win political status through the weight of public opinion. I disagreed with this. I pointed out to him that, as far as I could see, outside of our immediate families, the public was apathetic to the protest. As well as that, I posed the question: what strategic alternative did the British have if they were to abandon their stance on the prison issue? Their whole Ulsterisation policy hinged on it because they could not credibly claim that a criminal conspiracy was taking place on the streets and country lanes of the North while prisoners were sitting in cells with nothing but a blanket around them, proclaiming to the world that they were political prisoners. We looked at the options – and there weren't too many of them. I told Blute that, in my opinion, this protest would eventually come down to a hunger strike, and I wasn't confident that hunger striking would succeed, given that the British must have allowed for such a development.

'You're being too pessimistic, Rick.'

'I hope you're right, Blute – for all our sakes.'

'Keep the faith, my son, keep the faith. The 'RA will win in the end.'

I loved Blute: he was always good for morale. Even during internment, he had refused to give in to depression. I wished at that moment that I had even a quarter of his faith, but I recognised that faith alone wouldn't save us this time. The future that I envisioned held little promise of victory; instead, I saw our spirits and hopes being ruthlessly tested in a battle of wills that would see us pitted against the might of the British government, armed with nothing but our willingness to endure hardship and possibly die for our beliefs.

The next day, we were moved to B-Wing to join the other protesters. Fortunately, I was still in the cell with Dollhead, and that was a definite bonus. He was a comforting influence on me, someone to whom I could confide my inner emotions, and someone who knew the pain of being separated from a wife and child.

Later that day, Bernie visited me. She was a bit low and was still trying to come to terms with my eight-year sentence. I told her it would fly by, but I was devastated for her. I couldn't even tell her when I would be released, because every day on the blanket protest was a day lost in the remission of my sentence. (In the British penal system, the prison governor has the legal right to withdraw remission/lieu of sentence if a prisoner breaks or does not obey prison rules. Remission is time off one's sentence for good behaviour. In the north of Ireland, a prisoner who had never been in trouble with the prison authorities could expect to serve only half of the sentence that had been handed to him by the courts. In our case, every day on the protest was a day longer in jail.) God alone knew when I would be able to resume my role as a husband and father and provide comfort and support for Bernie and our daughter. The huge guilt that I had felt about not telling her I was back in the IRA seemed to have multiplied. That night I prayed that she would be forgiving.

While it was obvious that there was a fearsome spirit of resistance amongst the protesting republican prisoners, it was also plain to see that the blanket protest was in danger of becoming an end in itself. The lads were made of solid rock, but solid rock alone wasn't going to be enough: the Blanketmen needed a source of hope, a more intensive sense of active resistance to the regime.

Chance lent a hand and our fortunes improved when six experienced men were shifted down from the Cages in January 1978, after they had been in a fight with some screws. Among this new group was Brendan Hughes, known affectionately as 'The Dark'. He had been the Officer Commanding (OC) of the Cages and Brigade OC of Belfast before his capture. (Those men who had been sentenced before 1 March 1976 were still afforded political status and were housed in another part of Long Kesh. There they saw out their sentences in Nissen huts enclosed within a wire perimeter fence. The authorities called a collective enclosure a 'compound', while we referred to them as 'cages'.) The Dark was a small, ascetic man, with a mop of black hair (hence his nickname), and he was very quiet and contemplative, with an awesome reputation amongst republicans. The Dark became OC of the Blanketmen and was to play a vital role in the development of the protest over the next three years.

Towards the end of March 1978, we went on the offensive and embarked on a 'no wash' protest. The idea was the result of discussions between The Dark, Bobby Sands and Tom 'Nail-bomb' McFeely from north Derry. The experiences of Jimmy Boyle, a Scottish lifer, were the wellspring for this tactic. To evade constant beatings from his jailors, Boyle, who had angrily protested his innocence of a murder charge, smeared shit on the walls and on himself. This had proved a very effective course of action. The point of our protest was to make conditions in the wings so appallingly unhygienic that sympathy for our plight would grow throughout Ireland.

To garner that sympathy, our internal leadership believed that we had to be seen as the helpless victims of screw pettiness and brutality who had been left with no choice but to go on a dirty protest, when in fact it was our intention to engineer those conditions. That wasn't as difficult as it sounded: we knew that we could rely on the screws to put the boot in. They revelled in any opportunity to degrade us, and what started off as our refusal to 'slop out' (empty our pisspots into a bucket at the cell door) escalated rapidly. A choreographed dance, reminiscent of the mating of crossbreeds, began. We refused to slop out, and the screws refused to come into the cells to empty our pisspots. We then threw our piss and shit out of the windows, and the screws hosed down the yard and soaked our cells. Then we smeared our shit on the cell walls and poured our piss under our cell doors. They would then brush the piss back into our cells and hose the inside of the wings, soaking our bedding. In the end, the screws introduced wing shifts, so that they could clean our cells with power hoses. These wing shifts became a source of dread because the screws used the occasion to beat us, even going so far as to randomly anal-search some Blanketmen. We in turn highlighted all this in the media.

The screws resented being obliged to enter our shit-filled world. As their impotence and fury at the new situation grew, they resorted to what screws everywhere know best: the wholesale use of brutality. And so the battle continued.

At the start, the no-wash protest was intensely difficult. I had grown a huge ginger beard and my hair was tumbling down my back, but not to wash was repugnant to me. After two weeks, my hair was in tats and sticking to my back with grease. I had great trouble with the smell of the rotting food – mostly cold porridge which we threw into the corner – and the shit that we smeared on the walls with pieces of foam torn from our mattresses. The more foam we tore from our mattresses, the smaller our sleeping area became, and we had to sleep in a fixed position because there was very little foam left. Dollhead and I would take turns at the window to breathe fresh air, while the other one paced the floor.

It was difficult not to feel like I was being buried alive in a sewer. The only escape was to abandon principles that were the nucleus of my being. I have to admit that at times I was tempted to put on the grey, woolen monkey suit that passed for prison clothing and run as far away from that stinking hellhole as I could.

Putting on the 'gear' was an attractive option: it was only a nod to a screw away. For a start, I would see Bernie and my daughter every week, instead of for thirty minutes once a month. Besides that, if I were to wear the prison uniform, I wouldn't be reeking of shit on their visit. Although Bernie tried her best to make me feel at ease, I had caught her involuntarily turning her head away in disgust at my rank smell. It was only years later, when the dirty protest had ended, that she admitted to me that I was surrounded by a 'vile stench'. I cringed on hearing that. How I must have appeared to her with my long hair, straggly beard and foul breath, wearing the monkey suit, while all around me were conforming prisoners wearing their own civilian clothes and smelling like roses in May. She must have been saying to herself that I could be neat and clean like them and counting the days to freedom, instead of adding to them by staying on the protest. At the very least, she must have been asking herself if this was the same man she had married a couple of years earlier.

I felt profound guilt at subjecting Bernie to this torment: she had done nothing to deserve this. By staying on the blanket, I was perpetuating her agony. If I came off the protest, the beatings would stop and I would lose no more remission and be with her, and our daughter Bernadette, all the quicker. I had only to give the nod.

In my heart of hearts, I knew that giving that nod to a screw was never really an option. I was torn between my political beliefs and loyalty to my comrades, and my love for and commitment to my wife. Either way, I was going to hurt other people; perhaps selfishly, I chose to hurt Bernie, the person I loved most in the world.

But it would be wrong to say that being on the blanket protest was all doom and gloom. There were some very amusing characters in our wing. Jimmy 'Teapot' McMullan, Gerard 'Geek' O'Halloran, Jim 'Hector' McNeill and Colm 'Scull' Scullion were prominent among the jailhouse wits. Teapot and Hector had formed an unofficial entertainment committee, and they organised nightly sing-songs and quizzes. Teapot's party piece was 'Skibbereen', a doleful song about the Irish

Famine of 1845–7. There are about two dozen verses to this song, and Teapot would sing every one of them – amid a chorus of raspberries and catcalls. Then there was Martin 'Hurson-Boy' Hurson, who hailed from County Tyrone. He was one woeful singer. When Hurson-Boy got up to the cell door to 'sing', the fake farting started even before he had opened his mouth. Not that he minded: wild horses and a dozen screws wouldn't have put him off. His offering was always 'Seán South from Garryowen', although if you hadn't an insider's knowledge, you wouldn't have had a clue what he was singing about. During a quiz, 'Scull', who came from Bellaghy, a rural village in south Derry, had taken on the role of quizmaster, and one of the questions he asked Hector was: 'How many tits does a sow have?' Hector's reply was that, if the sow had one tit, it would be one more than his girlfriend had.

Reciting poetry was another means of entertainment. I remember composing a derisive poem about a parliamentarian. After I'd finished reading it out the cell door, I waited for what I hoped would be a favourable reaction. Teapot started the giggling first, and then the whole wing joined in. The H-Blocks weren't a place for a sensitive soul: you had to learn quickly that nothing got in the way of the craic.

5

It was a choking summer day; there wasn't a breath of air in the cell, and the smell was abominable. A swarm of bluebottles buzzed about the rotten food piled up in the corner. I hated bluebottles; they and the seagulls, with their infernal buzzing and squawking, would awaken us at dawn every morning.

Dollhead and myself were playing chess on a board marked out on the floor, using little squares torn out of the Bible as chess pieces. Suddenly my eyes nearly popped out of their sockets, as I noticed that the rotten pile of food was moving. Dollhead saw it too and went to investigate. As he removed the outer layer of the decomposed food, little white insects started to emerge. Hundreds of them were wriggling their way to freedom!

The insects must have had a prearranged timetable for mobilisation, because they emerged together at exactly the same time all over the wing. Lads were shouting that their cells were infested with these creatures. Hurson-Boy informed the wing that they were maggots and had come from bluebottles laying their eggs in the rotten food.

Nothing had prepared me for this. Cleaky Clarke, the wing OC, ordered that the maggots weren't to be destroyed or interfered with in any way, but I made it clear to Dollhead that either the maggots went or I did. While I could take all that the screws threw at me, maggots were a different matter: these little guys had the potential to finish me off.

We found it harder to kill them than we had imagined, for even when we cut them in half they still wriggled about. Eventually, we mixed the pile of rotten food and the maggots together into a hard paste with water. We then scooped up small amounts of the paste on the lids of our pisspots and threw it onto the walls, where it stuck like glue.

Other men obeyed the order and woke up every morning with maggots in their hair and beards. How they could do that was beyond me. From then until the end of that summer of 1978, we made sure that any inedible food was mixed immediately and smeared on the wall.

The screws turned up the pressure and introduced the 'mirror search', during which they would force us to squat naked over a mirror on the floor to have our back passages searched. This happened every two weeks when we were moved to a clean wing or when we went to the visiting huts for our monthly visit. If you were lucky, the screws only pushed you down, but if you got a couple of bad bastards, they would take great pleasure in slapping you about the back of your head until they got tired or bored, and then they pushed you down. Beatings became routine in H-Block 3 as an all-out effort was made to break the spirits of the protesters. We were entitled to one visit a month and of course were overjoyed to see our families, but there was a terrible sense of apprehension because we knew that after the visit a tanking had been booked in for us in cell 26.

On one occasion, Kevin Lynch (whose nickname was 'Barabbas' because he looked like Barabbas in the movie *The Greatest Story Ever Told*) was informed by the medical officer that he had to ask the screws for salt to gargle with because his mouth had broken out in a mass of ulcers.

In spite of numerous calls, the screws ignored Barabbas, so in frustration he hit the emergency bell on the wall to get some attention. Within minutes, we could hear a dozen screws heading down the wing. The sound of so many boots meant only one thing.

'Did you ring that bell, Lynch?' Paddy Joe Kerr, the principal officer in the block, asked through the spy-flap.

'The MO . . . '

'Never mind the fuckin' MO. Did you ring that bell, Lynch?' Kerr always spoke in quiet, controlled tones, but behind his soft voice was a twentieth-century Javier, the despotic sleuth in Victor Hugo's *Les Miserables*. (Kerr was a Catholic, and because he was of the same religion as us, we reckoned that he believed he had to prove himself to be more brutal than his Protestant counterparts.)

'Yes,' said Barabbas.

'What do you want, Lynch?'

'Salt, PO. The MO told me to ask for salt to gargle my mouth out.'

'So you want salt, Lynch? It's your lucky day, my friend. It just so happens I've salt with me. Open the door, class officer.'

The words 'my friend' were said with such contempt that I cringed for Barabbas. He told us later that six screws had entered his cell and, as four of them pinned him down, the PO stood on his shoulders while another man pulled his chin and nose to force open his mouth. The PO then pushed two big handfuls of salt into the poor guy's mouth and made him dry-swallow it. With Barabbas almost choking, the PO relented and ordered that he be given water to help him digest the salt.

This wasn't an isolated case – and not even spectacular by H3 standards – but it illustrated the fact that no opportunity was missed. (Kerr was later shot dead by the IRA outside Armagh Cathedral after attending Mass. Fourteen prison officers met early and violent deaths for what had been done to republican prisoners in the H-Blocks.)

A former blanket screw, Pat McCusker, told Liam Clarke, author of *Broadening the Battlefield*, about the following incident:

> I said to Hughes [The Dark]: 'They were all wrong beating those boys, because if you think about it when they are locked up in the cell they had nothing to think about. They needed something to hold them together. What they had was hate. The officers played right into their hands. The Northern Ireland Office didn't know any psychology at all. They didn't know the make-up of who they were up against; the beatings they got just stiffened them as nothing else could.'

McCusker went on to say: 'What they [the screws] should have done was killed them [the Blanketmen] with kindness.' Here was a dangerous man! Kindness would have shown a disarming degree of apathy towards the dirty protest, which would have left us wondering why we had started it. Instead, we would have been forced to think of some way of intensifying the protest, such as smearing the shit on our own bodies. (One man actually advocated this.)

Years after we were released, Colm Scullion told me that he had met one of the less violent screws at a country fair and that both men had recounted their experiences of the dirty protest. Scull told me that the screw had said to him: 'If you lads had known what was going into your food after it arrived in the blocks from the prison cookhouse, youse would have been on hunger strike earlier. It was a wonder none of you suffered from food poisoning or had jaundice.'

As conditions got worse, there was a corresponding deterioration in some men's health. Francie Hanvey, who was in the cell next to us, was vomiting up tiny tapeworms, dozens of them at a time. The MO had prescribed him tablets to control the tapeworms, but these had no effect; the worms just kept on coming up. Other prisoners had continuous diarrhoea, and one prisoner was already in hospital after having a mental breakdown caused directly by the protest. (This man died several years after he was released. It was said that he never recovered from his ordeal.)

It was noticeable that our brutal protest was affecting people in different ways. Even though we were surrounded by comrades, loneliness and dejection were always close at hand for any of us. You needed an inordinate amount of inner discipline and strength to rise above the prevailing insanity. The discipline that was essential for survival was founded not only in the justice of our cause, but also in the loyalty and affection we had for each other. But as we drifted inexorably into more extreme forms of protest, it became impossible for us to grasp the severity of our own degradation; it was as if the protest itself had become a living entity.

It was only when 'Cool' Eddie Fay, a fellow prisoner, said, during a discussion out the cell doors, that we didn't even realise the nature of the conditions we were enduring that the reality of it all hit me. I thought long and hard about what Eddie had said and came to the conclusion that he was right: we were enveloped in a shit-covered bubble of protest, an ugly world where nothing else existed, where the affairs of the outside world were of little relevance as we fortified our spirits to face the immediate challenge of surviving each day, to win through somehow. If anyone had told me before I had gone on protest that I would end up smearing shit on walls and throwing piss out the doors, I would have told them they were round the bend.

At the end of 1978, word came down to us that the authorities had decided to forcibly wash and shave us. We knew that this would probably entail a good thumping, and there was an air of despondency on the wings.

The night before this was to happen, we established communication with H5, which was about two hundred yards from us, by shouting over to them and informing them about the plan to force-wash us the next day. The Dark and the rest of the leadership were in H5. There was silence at the other end for quite a while. Then a voice shouted, '*Buailigí orthu*' ('Fight them'). Hack Smith was in the next cell and he tapped the pipes immediately. 'Did I hear right, Rick?' he asked.

'Ya did, Hack. We've to get into the screws tomorrow mornin' when they try to force-wash us.'

'Oh fuck, no!'

Hack wasn't the only one who was having rickets at the prospect of a good shoeing. What was being proposed was nothing short of suicide. Big Cleaky shouted to the voice to repeat the last order, and again we were told: '*Buailigí orthu*.' Cleaky asked everyone on the wing if we could make out what was being shouted and was met with silence. There was another shout to their wing. This time they all shouted back the same order, and again Cleaky pretended to be deaf. After a while, the lads in H5 got H4 to shout over as well – just in case we really hadn't heard – and both blocks shouted in unison: '*Buailigi orthu!*' We still pretended not to hear them. If they had got the whole of the Belfast Brigade to shout that order, we would have pretended not to hear it.

Then one voice in our wing spoke up: 'They're tellin' us to get into the screws tomorrow mornin'.' The voice belonged to Blute McDonnell, who had urged me to 'Keep the faith, my son, keep the faith' and told me that 'The 'RA will win in the end' after I had given him my pessimistic view of the protest. I had always valued Blute as a good republican and friend, but at that moment I would joyfully have strangled him; and yet I was scarcely surprised at his intervention, given his reverence for IRA procedures.

He and I were hardly strangers to beatings from prison authorities. When I had been interned for a second time in 1973, I was incarcerated in the same hut as the indefatigable Blute. During that period, we were both on the receiving end of a severe beating from the British soldiers who guarded the perimeter of Long Kesh. This came about because one of our comrades, Mark Graham, had tried to escape by secreting himself under the prison grub wagon. Two hours after the aborted escape, a large contingent of British soldiers entered Cage 3, ostensibly to do a search, and immed- iately ordered us to put up our hands against the outer wire fence of the cage. Our OC had told us not to comply with the British order. There were two British soldiers for every one of us, and the British commander ordered his troops to beat us about the elbows with their batons until we complied with the order. While some men eventually obeyed the order, I didn't, and was rewarded for my stubbornness by being selected, along with the OC and another man, for special treatment. The three of us were put up against Hut 22 and repeatedly hit with batons. After it was all over, everybody in the cage had the black-and-blue marks of resistance to show for their opposition, although some were more marked than others. If I remember right, Blute was particularly bruised. (Mark Graham was captured after he broke his back while the van was going over a ramp. He is now confined to a wheelchair.)

Meanwhile, back on the wing, Willie John McAllister, who had been sentenced with Dollhead and me, started shadow-boxing in his cell. This display of bravado put the fear of God into his cellmate. Such was the poor guy's terror that, at eight o'clock the next morning, when the screws opened the cell door to give him his breakfast, he walked out onto the wing and left the protest behind.

As events unfolded, our Block OC refused to accept the order on the grounds that H5 had no idea how damaging such a course of action would be to morale in the block. It was a courageous decision – and a very welcome one.

I approached the next morning with all the dread of one who had been ordered to leave the trenches and walk towards the machine-guns. My stomach churned when a screw shouted, 'Lock up!' After closing down the wing, the screws headed to the 'circle'. We all knew that the forced-washing would begin shortly. We had been ordered by the OC to sit on our beds, so that the screws would have to drag us out to the washrooms. Even that mild show of defiance might ensure a terrible retribution, however.

Heavy footsteps and the rattle of keys heralded the screws' return. I looked at Dollhead and saw that his lips were tightly pursed: he was mentally preparing himself for whatever lay ahead. I couldn't hold off; I needed to 'go' there and then. Dollhead laughed as I squatted in the corner, and he shouted in to Hector McNeill in Irish: 'McNeill, the shite's runnin' out of O'Rawe.' Hector shouted back: '*Ní nach ionadh.*' ('No wonder'.) He then told us that he had already been in the corner a couple of times himself.

Doors opened and the screws ordered us to get washed. Almost immediately, we heard men being dragged along the corridor. Soon our door opened and we received the order. A shake of the head told them that we were going nowhere. Four screws grabbed us by the legs and pulled us out of the cell and up the wing towards the washrooms.

When we reached the washrooms, I could see that there were dozens of screws waiting. I was dragged over to the bath. 'Get in.' I shook my head. 'Get into the fuckin' water, tramp.'

I lay still. At that, I was lifted up by four screws and tossed into the water. It was icy cold and I started to shiver violently. The screws laughed and the 'Ballymena Cowboy', a screw who enjoyed his job, started to scrub me with a deck brush. Its coarse bristles tore at my skin, but the ice-cold water insulated me to some extent.

I was only too happy to stand up and get out of the water when I was told to, and was manhandled across the washroom and set down on a chair. Another screw took a pair of shears and set about shaving my head and beard. I was naked and shivering uncontrollably. There was no finesse to his work: to him, I was just a piece of meat.

When it was all over, we counted the cost. Hurson-

Boy had two broken toes, Joe McNulty had a broken nose, Tomboy Loudon, with his black eye and cut head, looked like a character out of a horror movie, and others still had a few tufts of long hair sticking out at the side of their head or at the front. The screws must have thought that was funny.

When everyone was accounted for and safely in the new wing (with the exception of Hurson-Boy, who had been taken to camp hospital), someone started singing: 'Provos, march on!' Soon the whole wing was belting out the song, amid shouts of '*Tiocfaidh ár lá*' ('Our day will come'), the battle-cry of the Blanketmen. At that moment, I felt proud to be a Blanketman, proud to know such honourable comrades and proud to be part of a protest that was the bane of the British government's existence.

Word came through to us via the loyalist orderlies who served us our food that the screws were planning to isolate the leadership in an attempt to disrupt communications. The Block OC and Cleaky were certain to be moved, and it was agreed that, if this happened, I would become Block OC. I hadn't been involved in any leadership activities, so it was assumed that I would not be part of the move.

In February 1979, Cleaky's door opened and he was told he was being moved to another block. Almost simultaneously, keys rattled outside our door: I felt certain that the screws had found out that I was to take over as Block OC. My suspicions were confirmed when I was told I was moving too. Before I was whipped off to H6, along with thirty others, I just had time to leave word that Tomboy Loudon was to be the new Block OC.

A blood-red cloak was dropped on the H-Blocks in

the wake of the leadership's removal to H6. Psychological and physical torture were increased significantly on H3, H4 and H5, and an all-out offensive was mounted to break the spirit of the republican prisoners. Almost immediately, we were receiving reports of widespread, systematic beatings. It was obvious that the British government had given the screws *carte blanche* to do whatever was necessary to bring the protest to an end.

What the British administration had not taken into consideration was the spirit of resistance that beat inside the heart of every Blanketman. 'Teapot' McMullan had once summed it up for me when he said: 'It's not the size of the man in the fight that counts, but the size of the fight in the man.'

H6, meanwhile, was a relative holiday camp. There were very few beatings, and life was far from unpleasant, as the British implemented a policy of isolating the republican leadership from the rest of the republican prisoners. They were saying, in a roundabout way, to the other prisoners that their leaders were immune to their suffering and were living the life of Riley in H6. This was an attempt to cause disaffection among the prisoners, in the hope that some of them would hold the leadership in contempt. But our wing was vibrant. The Dark, Bobby Sands, Bik McFarlane, Larry Marley, Seanna Walsh and Blute, among others, added a touch of colour to the bleak reality of the twenty-four-hour lockup.

Bik, six feet tall and full of *bonhomie*, was a striking character. He had an assertive, reassuring manner and exuded confidence in his own ability to overcome adversity. Like myself, Bik was an avid Gaelic-football supporter, and he and I whiled away the time dreaming of the day when the Antrim football team would grace Croke Park in an All-Ireland final.

Bik was a great singer, and on many occasions he treated us to his vast repertoire of songs, which ranged from Joni Mitchell's 'Big Yellow Taxi' and Bad Company's 'Superstar' to Procol Harum's 'A Whiter Shade of Pale'. Sometimes, though, he would withdraw into himself and distance himself from the general routine. A deeply spiritual man, Bik found comfort in the Bible. During those periods, I used to quote a friend of mine, 'Fat' Campbell, whose favourite ditty was: 'Keep smilin' at troubles, 'cause troubles are bubbles, an' bubbles will soon blow away.' This usually elicited a bit of craic from Bik – even if was not always complimentary to Fat or myself!

Bobby Sands, on the other hand, never shut up. He was the life and soul of the wing. A charismatic individual, he had a soft, waxy-coloured face (the result of sunless years on protest) surrounded by long fair hair, and spoke with a slightly rasping voice. His most abiding qualities were his energy and effervescence. His influence was everywhere, and his enthusiasm was infectious.

An example of Bobby's spirit was the excerpts from books that he regaled us with on the wing at night-time. These were books he had read before he was sentenced and which he recalled with great accuracy. The tales were very entertaining, but they invariably contained at their core an element of struggle. Whether it was Wat Tyler and his army of a hundred thousand peasants rebelling against their feudal overlords in medieval England, or Geronimo, the Apache Indian chief fighting alone against the US army, or Spartacus and his fellow slaves resisting the might of Imperial Rome, the theme was always the same: the perennial battle between good and evil, between the underdog and the bully. To Bobby, the H-Block protest epitomised all the elements of those ancient struggles and was the highest form of altruism and dignity. For him, every Blanketman was a Spartacus.

Bobby was a tireless propagandist: in the H-Blocks he set about creating a propaganda factory that churned out communiqués. Tiny comms were smuggled in and out every day. Appeals for support were written on cigarette papers and smuggled out in the mouths, foreskins and noses of prisoners. Our people outside then sent these appeals to every major newspaper in the world, as well as to colleges, trade unions, prominent foreign politicians and anyone else who could help build sympathy for our cause. On top of this, Bobby Sands and Seanna Walsh started Irish classes on our wing.

Larry Marley had been caught with Bik and Pat Beag McGeown while trying to masquerade as screws to escape from the Cages in 1977. As a result, all three lost their political status and were sent to the H-Blocks. Larry had a dry wit. Some time during his stay in the Cages, he had read that it was possible for a person to leave their earthly body and travel to the astral plane, which he explained was a sort of halfway house between heaven and earth. After warning us that we might meet unsavoury spirits in this other dimension, and that we should hold on to our lifeline at all costs in order to return to our bodies, he tried to hypnotise us so that we could 'cross over'. I followed his instructions to the letter, but all that happened was that I fell asleep! (Larry was shot dead on 3 April 1987 by the UVF after answering his door in Ardoyne. Of the thirty-one men who were originally moved to H6, four are now dead, the others being Willie 'Deek' Johnston, Bobby and Tom McElwee. John George, who is also now dead, joined the protest after we were moved from our original blocks.)

Lectures on republicanism became a regular occurrence in the H-Blocks. For the first time in my involvement with the republican movement, I heard of the five 'ism's that constitute the republican philosophy: socialism, non-sectarianism, nationalism, secularism and separatism. The former Cage 11 men, The Dark, Bobby, Bik, Larry and Seanna, were at the forefront of this educational programme. (The messianic figure of Gerry Adams had been in Cage 11 until 1977, along with the five lads, and his underlying political outlook was the inspiration for the lectures.) It was an outlook that I greedily adopted as my own.

One of the more pertinent engagements on the wings involved a discussion out the doors about the direction of the protest and the absence of widespread support for it on the streets and in the corridors of power. These were initiated by both The Dark and Bobby and led to a multitude of suggestions. It was finally agreed that a national H-Block committee should be established to co-ordinate protest activity on the outside and that this committee should include influential people who may not necessarily have agreed with our politics. Bobby communicated our views to the outside leadership.

John 'The Governor G' George and Paul 'Pidgy' Pidgeon had been in the conforming blocks and had decided to throw off their monkey suits and go on the protest. As a result, they landed in our wing.

Georgie and I had been friends from our remand days in the Crum, and I knew from experience that a cool wind had blown into our lives – that Georgie would soon have us in stitches with his irreverent banter. The first thing he did was to call The Dark, the H-Blocks OC, up to the cell door and introduce himself.

'I'm John George, Dark, but ya can call me Georgie. Here's the craic from now on: you may run the blocks, I haven't a problem with that, but I run this wing. If I say there's no Irish, then there's no Irish. If I want a sing-song, then there's a sing-song. If I want a kip, then everybody's to be quiet. Are ya with me?' (Pidgy could be heard telling Georgie to shut up, but he was wasting his breath.)

'I'm with ya, Georgie,' replied The Dark. 'You're the big noise from now on, *mo chara*. You're the man.' I could hear The Dark chuckling.

'I like your style, Dark. Now who else is here? Syd [Seanna Walsh, a fellow Short Strand man], get up to the door,' and Georgie began a bout of slagging that lasted until teatime.

Georgie was moved into a cell with Jackie McMullan. Jackie started his daily exercise routine the day after Georgie was moved in. As Jackie began to blow hard, Georgie called Bobby up to the cell window and told him that he wanted to make a complaint. When Bobby asked him what it was, Georgie replied that he wanted a cell-swap because Jackie was stealing all the air in the cell and he couldn't breathe.

'I'm chokin', Bobby, I can't breathe,' Georgie whispered. Bobby, ever the alert public-relations officer, answered him: 'So are we all, Georgie, so are we all.'

Georgie disliked Blute. Perhaps it wasn't so much a dislike of the man, but rather the fact that Blute didn't take visits, or even put on the prison trousers to go to Mass on Sundays, which was compulsory. Georgie regarded Blute as super-staunch and therefore an oddball. When it was Georgie's turn to tell a story out the cell door, he invariably described the villain of the piece as 'a big, baldy, horrible-lookin' monster called "Bluton",' or, alternatively 'Blutor' or 'Blutnick'.

Blute wasn't the type to get easily annoyed, but he would have pretended he was. He promised Georgie that he was going to put the trousers on and go to Mass, just to beat the crap out of him. At the same time, Blute would have been laughing at Georgie's antics.

The Irish National Liberation Army shot Georgie dead in Belfast in 1984 after his release. It was said that the reason for his execution was that he had robbed a couple of grocery stores. In those days, life was cheap in the City of No Pity.

6

On 27 August 1979, the republican remand prisoners, who were in the wing opposite us in H-Block 6, shouted over that there had been an explosion in the seaside village of Mullaghmore, County Sligo, and that Lord Louis Mountbatten, who had been fishing on board his boat, the *Shadow V*, had been killed by the IRA. Then, hot on the heels of that news, reports came in that six British paratroopers had been killed at Narrow Water, near the seaside town of Warrenpoint, County Down. Soon the number was eight, then ten, and eventually the tally rose to eighteen.

There was elation throughout our wing at the news about the Paras and this was demonstrated by us beating our cell doors with our empty pisspots. The Paras had been ruthless and trigger-happy in their dealings with nationalists and republicans, and none of us had any sympathy for them, dead or alive. As I lay in bed that night, I heard a couple of the lads, farther up the wing, talking about how they had been on the march on Bloody Sunday 1972 when the Paras had murdered fourteen innocent people. They talked about the consequences of the Warrenpoint operation and concluded that the war had taken a turn for the better for the IRA, and that if this level of loss was sustained in the coming months, the British government would have to consider its position in the North.

I had my own thoughts about the Warrenpoint ambush. I thought that the law of the universe – the measure you give is the measure you get – was being enforced. My thoughts regressed to 9 August 1971, the day that internment without trial was introduced in British-occupied North of Ireland. I had been in the IRA only five months before internment, and fortunately for me I had not come up on the British security-services' scanner.

However, I had been a Volunteer in the IRA unit that had been stationed in the Springfield Park area on internment night. (Springfield Park was a nationalist street of mostly private dwellings which rubbed shoulders with the loyalist Springmartin estate.) That night, loyalists from the Springmartin estate had tried to invade the upper end of Springfield Park. Although I was not 'on site' at the time of the conflagration, other comrades were, and they opened fire above the heads of the loyalist mob and dispersed them.

Our parish priest, Fr Hugh Mullan, had earlier pleaded with the loyalist mob to stop attacking the houses at the top of Springfield Park. He had been stoned for his efforts. He was later shot dead while trying to administer the last rites to a man who had been shot while crossing an exposed piece of ground between Springfield Park and the adjoining Moyard estate. Another man, Frank Quinn, was also shot dead that night at the same spot. The man whom Fr Hugh had so courageously gone to help survived being shot, and he later stated that he believed that Fr Hugh had been shot by British soldiers who were firing from flats in Springmartin.

The British government denied that their troops had

fired the shots that killed Fr Hugh. This shooting featured in an inter-state case that the Irish government later brought against the British government at the European Court of Human Rights. The Irish government stated that 'he [Fr Hugh] was shot by British troops while administering the last rites to a wounded person and while carrying a makeshift flag of truce'.

In all, seven residents of the Greater Ballymurphy area were shot dead by British troops on 9 and 10 August 1971. It is generally accepted that the Paras were responsible for most of the killings. None of the residents were IRA Volunteers or were in any way connected to the republican movement.

I had another reason for hating the Paras; they had shot and seriously wounded my younger brother, Mick, on the morning of 9 September 1972.

The sky promised to deliver bucketfuls of rain on any unfortunate who cared to venture out. The proverbial cheque from America had arrived, sent by my mother's aunt Margaret, who lived in Chicago, and Mick and my nine-year-old sister, Susie, had left the house to get the cheque changed at Eastwood's Bookmakers at the top of the Whiterock Road. Along with the cheque, they were carrying a bag of washing for the launderette, which was around the corner from the bookie's.

Inside the house, I was finishing off a fry, hoping that the coast was clear because I had to go into Ballymurphy for a meeting. That venture had been put in doubt, though, because a fusillade of high-velocity shots had just been fired, and no doubt the Paras would be out in force. As I looked out the window, a Para was standing on the pavement looking directly into the house. He smiled when he saw me.

Within a short space of time, the Paras had left, and Terry McHugh, a family friend, came to the door with Susie to tell us that Mick had been shot by the Paras and taken away in a Saracen. My father asked Terry how badly he had been shot. Terry said he didn't know because the Paras wouldn't let anyone near Mick. Was Mick dead? The thought terrified me. Our wee Susie was in a terrible state. She told us that Mick had left her in the launderette and gone to the bookie's to get the cheque cashed. He told her he would be away for twenty minutes because he was going to Turf Lodge to see a friend. The next thing Susie knew, there was shooting and someone was shouting that Micky O'Rawe had been shot. She ran out onto the Whiterock Road and Alfie McAvoy grabbed her. Terry then brought her home. Mick was only fifteen years old, a big, straggly kid who was a threat to no one.

My father and I immediately made our way to the Whiterock Road. People told us that Mick had been shot while crossing Shepherd's Path, about a hundred yards from the top of the Whiterock, and that a lady called Mrs Mulholland had also been shot.

We immediately got a taxi to the Royal Victoria Hospital and were directed to the intensive-care ward. My mother, who worked in the hospital at the time, was sitting in the waiting area. She was very distressed. A friend had been trying to console her, but she was crying hysterically, repeating over and over, 'My Michael.'

My father approached a doctor, who told him that Mick had been shot four times, once in the back and three times in the legs. The doctor said that if Mick had reached the hospital ten minutes later, he would have been dead. He said that Mick was still 'critical' and that, if he recovered, he would be very ill for some time. Eventually, the doctors persuaded us that there was no point in us remaining in the hospital, and we went home.

We phoned the hospital every hour, and the news got better as the day progressed. The operation had been a success, and Mick was expected to make a good recovery – although we were cautioned that he wasn't out of the danger zone, and there was a possibility that he would never walk again without the aid of a walking stick.

That night, a group of Paras were whooping it up outside our house. They began singing: 'Where has Micky gone? Far, far away.' We ignored their taunts, but I remember thinking to myself that some day the shoe would be on the other foot. I prayed that, when that day came, it would be my finger that was pulling the trigger or making the connection on the bomb that would blow them to smithereens.

In a statement to the press immediately after Mrs Mulholland and Mick had been shot, the Paras alleged that Mick was a gunman who had aimed a pistol at them. They also said that Mrs Mulholland had come to his aid and had removed the pistol. Yet she was shot also, and was lying wounded beside him, so she couldn't have removed any gun. When they realised how implausible their story was, the Paras released a second statement, saying that Mrs Mulholland wasn't the woman who had removed the gun after all, and that the culprit had escaped. They were making up stories on the hoof. The next day, sixty-five Catholic priests issued a statement condemning the indiscriminate shooting of 'innocent and unarmed civilians, regardless of age or sex'.

We visited Mick the morning after he had been shot. The staff in the intensive-care unit told us that he had regained consciousness during the night and had been taken to a private room off one of the wards. His left leg was in traction and his speech was slurred, but he managed to tell us what had happened.

He had been crossing Shepherd's Path to get to his friend's house. The next thing he knew, he was flying through the air and felt as if he was being hit with sledgehammers. He vaguely remembered Mrs Mulholland, who was passing by, being hit as well. Then he remembered looking up and seeing Paras surrounding him threatening to finish him off. He reckoned that they would have killed him if Mrs Mulholland hadn't been there to witness everything. Mick said that the Paras had thrown him into a Saracen armoured car and driven around west Belfast, deliberately not taking him to the hospital right away. When they were doing this, they were beating him and poking their rifles into the bullet holes. I asked Mick how long it had taken them to get him to hospital, but he couldn't remember: all he knew was that it seemed to be forever, and he passed out before the journey was over.

Fortunately, Mick eventually made a complete recovery, as did Mrs Mulholland, who, along with Mick, was given substantial compensation at a later date. The crux of the matter, though, was that no one was charged with the two shootings. There wasn't even a hint of an apology from the British army, or a statement saying that a mistake had been made. But then again, we didn't expect the Paras, who, it seemed to the republicans, had been given medals for murdering fourteen people in Derry, to be brought to book over a non-fatal shooting in Ballymurphy.

If Mrs Mulholland or Mick had died, the situation would have been no different: no one would have had to answer for the deaths. The rule of law meant nothing in Ballymurphy or the Bogside. The British military hierarchy needed 'kills' to show that they were winning the war, and the Paras were the boys to provide those kills.

The death of Lord Mountbatten had been greeted with some euphoria in our wing: many of us took the view that, as a member of the royal family, he was a legitimate target. This jubilation was tempered, however, when we found out that his fourteen-year-old grandson, Nicholas Knatchbull, and Paul Maxwell, a fifteen-year-old schoolboy from County Armagh who had taken a summer job as Lord Mountbatten's boatman, had also died. Another victim of the explosion, eighty-two-year-old Lady Patricia Brabourne, had died of her injuries in Sligo Hospital the day after the attack. Unlike the elation I had felt on hearing of the ambush of the Paras (whom I regarded as my enemy and a bunch of bloodthirsty killers of innocent people), I found nothing to cheer about in the killing of this elderly lady and two innocent schoolkids. The consensus in the wing was that Lord Mountbatten's death would rock the British establishment to the core. Still, I personally thought that, as an operation, it had a stink about it. I have always felt that killing non-combatants was unacceptable, even if they were members of the British royal family (although republicans could argue that they were combatants, given their titular positions as commanders of various British regiments, the most obvious example being Prince Charles, who was, and is, colonel-in-chief of the Parachute Regiment). No matter about the rights and wrongs of killing Lord Mountbatten, I could see no justification, or moral precedent, for the calculated and indiscriminate taking of three innocent people's lives.

Putting my own misgivings about the attack on Mountbatten to one side, a corollary of the dramatic upsurge in IRA activity was the feeling among us that the new IRA leadership, which had emerged in the wake of the disastrous 1975 ceasefire – when we had allowed ourselves to be sucked into sectarianism and feuding with other republicans – were brilliant strategists. The Gerry Adams/Ivor Bell-led overthrow of the 'Old Brigade' who had pursued that ceasefire seemed to have been vindicated. This, in conjunction with the leftist turn that Adams and Bell were advocating and their obvious militancy, led us to believe that we had a leadership in place that would deliver the Republic of our dreams. For the first time since 1972, I felt we were winning the war and that the British were defeatable.

Later that night, my cellmate, Flash McVeigh, and I naturally mulled over the momentous events that had occurred earlier in the day. We reckoned that Lord Mountbatten's death was more politically significant than those of the eighteen Paras. It certainly appeared so, given the emphasis that his death received in the radio reports in comparison to those of the Paras.

Flash had little experience of the Paras because he lived in the Beechmount area of the Falls Road and the Paras hadn't been stationed there, but he was interested in hearing of their behaviour when they were in Ballymurphy in 1972. I explained that one of their major tactical objectives had been to fragment and isolate the Ballymurphy community and so cause mass disorientation among the people. They did this through a well-thought-out campaign of terror that involved the use of brutality against anyone they caught in the streets – whether they were known IRA members or not. Another aspect of this tactic was the 'screening' (arrest and interrogation) of the entire male population over the age of sixteen to extract any possible information they might have about IRA activity. In instances where the Paras suspected that a person in their custody had information that they were concealing, their intelligence officers consistently resorted to beatings to draw out that information. The beatings varied from slapping someone about to outright torture, and depended on the quality of the suspect's perceived information and the level of resistance they offered. Obviously, an IRA Volunteer had more information than a civilian; therefore, he could expect a greater beating.

Flash asked me if I had been beaten. I told him of an incident that had happened to me when the Paras took me to the Black Mountain army base in the loyalist Springmartin estate in 1972.

I had been taken out of a black taxi and arrested by the army at the Children's Hospital on the Falls Road. They held me until a platoon of Paras came from Black Mountain Barracks to collect me. This was extraordinary because I was staying at home, and they could have come for me at any time.

They took me to the barracks, and I noticed that the base was packed as usual. (I had been there on numerous occasions before.) Within minutes, though, all the other suspects were being released. It suddenly dawned on me that the barracks had been emptied for me: the dubious distinction of the five-star treatment was about to be bestowed on me.

I was placed in a cubicle, and a Para, one of the biggest bastards I had ever seen, entered the room and hit me the most tremendous slap on the side of my face. When I picked myself up off the floor, he made me stand against the wall with one fingertip of each hand touching the wall and only my toes touching the ground. He then proceeded to punch me, making sure not to mark my face.

'Admit you're in the IRA and I'll let you go,' he demanded.

'Mister, I don't know what you've heard, but I'm not in the IRA.'

He didn't like that answer and set about taking mighty swings at my ribs. Every time I collapsed, he lifted me like a puppy and continued where he had left off.

'Before you and I part, my friend, you'll be begging to tell me about the IRA. You were on a snipe today in New Barnsley Drive, weren't you? Trying to kill us, you fucking IRA bastard. Where's Jim Bryson? Who was with you today?'

Another interrogator, a little fellow, joined him, and together they played the drums on my ribs. After a while, I felt myself becoming physically weaker; my fingers and toes were aching and my ribs were so sore I was having difficulty breathing. It was impossible to maintain the spread-eagle position for more than a few minutes at a time. Each time I collapsed, they picked me up, but the more they tortured me, the more I convinced myself that I wasn't in the IRA and that this was all a colossal mistake.

Another Para was sweeping the corridor outside the room, and the big guy took the brush off him and told him to get lost. I didn't like the way this was shaping up. After another fall, they stood me up facing them and the big one said: 'This is your last chance to come clean, O'Rawe. If you don't admit you're in the Provisionals, I'm going to shove this brush up your arse.'

I repeated what I had said before, and they once again turned me to the wall. The little guy opened my trousers and pulled them and my underpants to my ankles. 'Last chance, O' Rawe. Tell me who was on that snipe with you today, or I'm going to ram this brush up your fucking arse.'

I made no reply. While the big guy held up my hands, his compatriot pushed the brush into my anus. I screamed in agony as it was pushed farther into me. While the pain was excruciating, the humiliation was even worse. I felt the brush begin to move up and down inside me. By this time, I'm sure that the people who lived outside the barracks could hear my screams. The whole gory thing probably lasted less than a minute, but it seemed to go on forever. I fell again, and the brush jerked, making the pain that I had experienced before pale into insignificance. As I lay on the floor, I felt a warm sensation at the back of my legs of liquid running from my back passage. I realised that it must be blood.

The two Paras looked down at me, beads of sweat glistening on their foreheads. I was overwhelmed with the desire to sleep; my eyes felt almost too heavy to stay open. An officer entered the room and told my tormentors to 'Fuck off.' On the way out the door, the big Para said: 'Y'know, Reggie, I don't think this cunt's in the IRA after all.' Reggie burst out laughing.

I was soon released – thrown out of a Saladin armoured car at the top of the Whiterock Road. I made my slow way home. Once there, I showed my parents the bruises and told them about the brush episode. It was all we could do to stop my father going out and punching the first Para he encountered.

'Jesus! That's powerful, Rick,' said Flash, his mouth open in amazement. 'I knew the Paras were rough, but I didn't think they were that bad.'

'There was worse than that, Flash. Some of the boys in the 'Murph left Black Mountain with their balls the size of cookin' apples. Frankie Cahill had a towel wrapped around his head an' water poured over it. He said that when this happened, he felt as if he was drownin'. I'll tell ya, Flash, there'll be no tears in the 'Murph tonight over those dead Paras, that's for sure.'

Sometimes things happen that you remember all your life. The dark nights were creeping in, and the screws had just left the wing after doing their final headcount. Flash had just finished about two hundred press-ups and was sitting on his bed. I was standing at the window getting some air.

'All right now, baby, it's all right now . . .' Bik drummed on the grille on the window, keeping perfect time with his song. I joined in: 'It's all right, it's all right, it's all right . . .'

Flash jumped up and joined me at the window, immediately taking on the role of lead guitar, while Bob adopted the bass-guitar part: 'Bomp, bomp, bomp bomp bomp, bomp . . .'

The boys were in full swing: 'It's all right, it's all right, it's all right . . .' 'Bomp, bomp, bomp bomp bomp, bomp . . .' 'All right now . . .'

It went on and on. Who needed instruments when your soul was on fire? Twenty minutes later, we were up there in the clouds, as free as the lark that would come to symbolise the writings of Bobby Sands. Did the band Free pen 'All Right Now' just for us? We didn't need alcohol or drugs or any other stimulant: we had each other and our spirits.

Bik, entertainer extraordinaire, asked us what was on the headstone of Paul Kossoff, the lead singer of Free, who had died at the age of twenty-five on 19 March 1976. After a dozen wild guesses, he told us: 'Paul, All Right Now.' So were we.

7

When the Brits saw that their efforts to isolate the republican leadership were not reaping the dividends they had expected, they changed tack and sent us back amongst the mainstream prisoners. The Dark, Bob, Bik, Seán 'Greener' Chillingworth, Jake Jackson, Big Tom McElwee and myself were moved to the same wing in H3.

When I entered Cell 26, a reception committee of six screws was waiting for me. I knew another beating was coming my way. Although I had become hardened, I still tensed in expectation of the first blow.

One of the group was a notorious screw with a maniacal hatred of the Blanketmen. After I had removed my prison trousers – the only garment we had worn during the transfer – he ordered me to bend over a mirror in order to see between the cheeks of my backside. I refused. Along with his buddies, he tore into me, punching my kidneys and slapping me, calling me a tramp. For those few minutes, I didn't know where I was. What bothered me wasn't so much the pain as the feeling of not being in control, of being a toy in their violent hands.

At the end of the beating, he had a red face and nose. 'Welcome back to H3, O'Rawe,' he said. 'The holiday's over.' The rest of the lads got the same treatment. Eventually they worked their way through the seven of us, and then I was placed in a cell with The Dark.

We soon found out how dire the morale of the prisoners was. After enjoying the relaxed regime of H6, being in H3 was like being abandoned on the dark side of the moon. I knew from experience that systematic beatings were the norm there, but when we were transferred, it was clear that the situation had markedly deteriorated, and horrific beatings were now occurring almost every hour.

We were told that those who took a visit were still guaranteed a beating. When the prisoners returned, they would refuse to squat over the mirror, and two screws would take turns slapping them about the ears until they got tired. Although this had been normal before I went to H6, the beatings had worsened considerably. The boys in the wing would try to count the number of slaps received before the screws finally forced the returning prisoner down over the mirror. The 'record', which Paddy McBride proudly held, was something like sixty-one. (Paddy was later shot dead when a deranged Peeler called Allen Moore went berserk, shooting him and two others in the Sinn Féin offices in Belfast on 4 February 1992. Moore then drove to Ballinderry, on the outskirts of Belfast, where he put the barrel of his legally held shotgun into his mouth and pulled the trigger.)

I experienced the intensified violence on my first day back in H3 when Bernie visited me. The visit hadn't gone well. Bernie was almost at breaking point with the protest. The constant worry of not knowing when it was going to end was taking its toll. She had had to learn to survive, to make far-reaching decisions on her own, to struggle with the perpetual problem of poverty – and to rear our daughter into the bargain. She understood the rationale behind the protest, but she was finding it difficult to keep up her spirits and maintain hope. For the first time, I felt that she was on the verge of asking me to wear the prison uniform and to return to her and our daughter, or else – although she never said this in as many words. I had always had a dread of that happening. If she gave me an ultimatum, all I could do was try and bolster her spirits by assuring her that it would be all over shortly, we would get back our full remission, and I would be out to her sooner than she thought. There were tears in her eyes when I told her that: not tears of joy, though, but tears of disbelief, of betrayal and of un-bridled anger.

As I walked back to H3, the last thing on my mind was the beating that awaited me. My heart was in turmoil: my wife was going through hell, and there was nothing I could do about it except countenance a sacrifice – abandoning the protest and my comrades – that would destroy me.

Two screws were waiting for me. I took off the prison gear that we had to wear for visits, went over to the mirror and waited for the pageant of brutality to begin.

'Bend.'

I stood still.

'I love this job,' one said, and immediately began slapping me as hard as he could on the back of my head with his open hand. As the blows rained down, the nursery rhyme 'One potato, two potato, three potato, four' came into my head. After about 'ten potatoes', I lost count, and my ears were ringing; after twenty, I was in agony, and by thirty, I was ready to bend. Fortunately my resolve held, and they had to push me down over the mirror. I was a relieved man when I saw The Dark's welcoming face as they led me into the cell.

That night, The Dark called a meeting of the prisoners at the cell doors. He and I looked at each other in dismay as we listened to a more detailed account of the beatings. These men had stood firm under a continuous bombardment, but it was obvious that morale was at an all-time low, and the more experienced men spoke for the rest when they said that they were nearly at the end of their tether. They had been on protest for about three years and had been locked up in Bastille-like conditions. They had endured the no-wash protest for almost two years, had been beaten black and blue on a daily basis and had been shorn like sheep. They were unbroken, but they were certainly weary.

It was evident that we were in a crisis and that, if that night's discussion was reflective of the way the republican prisoners in the other Blocks felt, the future of the protest was in jeopardy. The Dark promised to think deeply about what had been said.

Within a couple of days, he gave the order that we were to bend during the mirror search, and so the 'excuse' for beating us was removed. Morale lifted appreciably as the beatings decreased, and soon the storytelling and the Irish classes were in full swing once more.

I liked being in the cell with The Dark. He was a remarkable man who had had an interesting career in the IRA. He had been interned in 1973 at the age of twenty-five after being captured, along with Gerry Adams and Tom Cahill, at a meeting on the Falls Road. At the time, the British alleged that these three men, along with Ivor Bell, formed the nucleus of the Belfast Brigade staff of the IRA. The Dark managed to escape from internment by hiding in a rubbish lorry. Upon his release, he became OC of the Belfast Brigade; seven months later, he was arrested in the affluent Malone Road area, where he had rented out a flat while posing as a businessman. When his flat was searched, it was found to contain an assortment of weapons and, more strikingly, a set of documents outlining what the IRA's response in Belfast would be in the event of civil war breaking out. The press labelled these documents 'the doomsday plans'. The Dark was sentenced to fifteen years.

When in Cage 11 of Long Kesh, The Dark formed a pressure group, along with his old friends Gerry Adams and Ivor Bell. This triumvirate was very critical of the then IRA leadership for calling the 1975 ceasefire. After a fracas with some screws in Cage 11, The Dark was sentenced to another five years. Since this offence had occurred after the 1 March cut-off date, he was sent, along with six other men, to the H-Blocks. Shortly after that, he became OC of the protesting prisoners.

The Dark was the quiet, contemplative sort who rarely rushed into decisions. Sometimes he would sit on his bed for up to two hours staring into space; on these occasions, I knew to leave him alone because it was obvious that he was deep in thought. On other occasions, he could be very witty. One such occasion occurred when one of the many priests, who had just been to the Cages, visited us in our cell. It was customary for the priest to bring with him a parcel from our comrades in the Cages (who still had political status). In that parcel would be three or four ounces of tobacco, flints to light the roll-ups, pens, texts in Irish, miniature editions of the *Republican News*, stretch-and-seal wrapping (used to insulate whatever went up our bums) and some personal correspondence for The Dark. Sometimes there would even be a sweet or two, but the rest of the wing weren't told about that. (After all, we deserved something for our efforts.) When the priest left, we knew we had only a few minutes to hide the contents of the parcel before the screws did a cell search, because they suspected that the priest habitually carried 'contraband' in to us. I reached for a slab of butter, which we always kept on a clean part of the wall – in case of emergencies – and slapped it onto my bum. I then pushed most of the parcel 'home', leaving The Dark with hardly anything to hide. We had barely finished when 'Fat Jack' Girvan opened the door to start his cell search, putting us into 'Geek' O' Halloran and Gerard Clarke's cell.

At the end of the search, we returned to our cell and Fat Jack remarked: 'There'll be no tobacco handed over on my shift, Dark.' A sad-faced Dark replied: 'One thing about ya, Jack, ya don't miss much. It's hard to get past ya.' Fat Jack just smiled and wobbled away, his legs labouring under the weight of his enormous belly, happy with The Dark's acknowledgement that he was a hard nut to crack. Little did Fat Jack know that when he had put us out of the cell the tobacco had gone with us! When we returned, The Dark remarked 'It's hard to get one past Fat Jack, Rick' and went into a fit of laughter.

It's difficult to describe the feeling of getting one over on the screws. The rest of the wing, especially the smokers, loved to hear the priest coming into our cell. It meant a night of luxury, a night when they could smoke 'bishops' – large roll-ups – instead of the usual 'holy rolls', so called because at the start of the protest, when 'skins' (tobacco paper) were scarce, the smokers used the paper from the *Saint Martin de Porres* magazine as a substitute. (It was estimated that a 'bishop' equalled five 'holy rolls'.)

After the screws had done their final headcount, we got the parcels down, opened them up and examined the goods. The Dark nonchalantly commented that I could get 'an articulated lorry' up my arse and the screws wouldn't know, as he rolled himself a bishop. We then sent the goods up the wing through a little aperture in the heating pipes that ran along each side of the wing. Bobby was usually the man who distributed the tobacco. Jake Jackson, who had a photographic memory, always got the texts in Irish and read them immediately, in case the screws found them. That night, as the screws came to brush the piss out of the door at the bottom of the wing (we threw it under the cell doors at eight-thirty every night), they were met with a cloud of smoke as the smokers blew their fumes through their cell doors to infuriate them.

The Dark and I had many interesting discussions at night. He felt that the 1975 ceasefire had almost destroyed the IRA. In his opinion, the British had been stringing the IRA leadership along during the ceasefire by deceiving them into thinking that they (the British) were sincere when they said that they intended to withdraw from the North at some unspecified time in the future. In his view, the only thing on the minds of the British policy-makers was creating conditions whereby they could proceed with their policy of Ulsterisation and criminalisation. He went on to point out that the IRA seemed to be more concerned with killing Protestants during the ceasefire than with killing British soldiers, and this was sectarian and anti-republican. The Dark also felt that the prolongation of the ceasefire had led to a situation where it had been almost impossible to restart the campaign. Lastly, he ripped the 1975 leadership apart for initiating a feud with the Stickies (the Official IRA). He said that, not only did that fiasco alienate the IRA from elements of our support base, it also contributed to the British criminalisation policy by giving them the opportunity to say to the world that we were a bunch of criminals who thought nothing of killing our rivals.

All this made sense. But I had been one of the three OCs in the Greater Ballymurphy area at the time of the ceasefire and had assembled around me a formidable company of seasoned men. These men had been either interned or sentenced in Long Kesh and were extremely committed to the armed struggle. Like The Dark, I also felt the frustration of that period, of going to Battalion 'call-houses' (a call-house is a meeting place, usually in a house or flat, where IRA business is discussed) and of asking where we were going with this ceasefire, only to be told that the leadership knew what they were doing and that we needed to be patient.

I disagreed with The Dark's view that the IRA was almost defeated, though. I could speak only from a local perspective, but in Ballymurphy, with a glut of good men and women at our disposal, we never felt that we were staring into the face of defeat. Equally, at the daily Battalion call-house meetings, I met the OCs from the other companies in west Belfast, and never once did I leave with the impression that they thought we were on the verge of being defeated.

The Dark countered by saying that my assessment was based on local conditions and that I was unaware of the bigger picture. That was true, but at least I had hands-on experience of what was happening on the ground in the Second Battalion area of Belfast, which vied with south Armagh as the most active battalion area in the North.

The discussion with The Dark was prominent in my mind when, after I was released, I met Billy McKee. McKee had been OC of the Belfast Brigade at the time of the 1975 ceasefire, as well as being a member of the then seven-man IRA Army Council. He was a legendary figure in the IRA. He had played a pivotal role in forming the Provisional IRA in January 1970 and had also been involved in the defence of the Falls Road during the 1969 pogrom, when loyalists and B Specials (an auxiliary police force whose sole purpose was to defend the statelet of Northern Ireland) launched vicious attacks on the area around Divis Street and the Kashmir Road, where they burned whole streets to the ground. McKee had also been seriously wounded while defending Saint Matthew's Chapel in the Catholic Short Strand area in 1970. And in 1972, he led the hunger strike that won us political status in the first place.

I put The Dark and Gerry Adams's views on that ceasefire to McKee. He told me that during an Army Council meeting that he had attended in late 1974, Seamus Twomey (another veteran republican from the 1940s' and 1950s' campaign, and also a former OC of the Belfast Brigade) casually commented that a contact from the British government had suggested a ceasefire. As the Army Council moved on to other business, McKee asked Twomey to elaborate on the ceasefire suggestion. After hearing more about it, he persuaded the Army Council that it had a duty to suss out the nature of the contact before making a judgment on the proposal. He told me that he believed that a ceasefire would allow the IRA time 'to recuperate'. One reason it needed the ceasefire was that there was no money to finance the campaign. (It is estimated that it took £1 million sterling a year for the IRA to keep the war going.) Another factor in favour of the ceasefire was that the IRA was almost unable to function militarily because of security-force arrests of active Volunteers. Outside of south Armagh, most IRA volunteers were in jail. (I remember that, before my arrest on the charge of conspiring to murder, there were only about six active Volunteers in Ballymurphy; after the ceasefire, there were enough men to form three companies, owing mainly to the release of internees from Long Kesh.) A further consideration was that there were very few weapons about. The combination of a penniless republican movement, few active Volunteers on the ground to pursue the war and the dire lack of gear made the prospect of replenishing all three during the lull created by a ceasefire an attractive proposition.

The crux of McKee's position, however, was that, as time went on, he became more and more convinced that the armed struggle hadn't the potential to force the British to leave Ireland, and therefore it should be wound up on the most favourable terms possible. According to The Dark, he, Adams and Bell suspected that this was McKee's viewpoint. This, and some fatal mistakes on McKee's part – the feud with the Stickies being a prime example – explains the overthrow by Adams and Bell of the McKee leadership in Belfast in 1977, after Adams and Bell were released from Long Kesh. It also explains their ascendancy to the leadership of the republican movement, the reorganisation of the IRA from large-company formations into small, more security-conscious cell structures and the promotion of the 'long war' strategy (a strategy that was, in retrospect, fatally flawed because it contained within its title an admission that the war was going nowhere). The consequences of the rise to power of Adams and Bell in the republican movement were a more vigorous campaign and a militancy that brought with it a promise that never again would we call a ceasefire unless the British gave us a timeframe within which they would agree to withdraw from the North. That was music to my ears.

The irony is that, like McKee, Adams, if not Bell, was pragmatic enough to realise the limitations of the armed-struggle approach; hence the 'long war' strategy. But while Adams recognised that the war could not be won militarily, he also saw that simply to call it off would have made the republican movement directionless and politically irrelevant. Not only would calling the war off have left us in the political wilderness, but also it would have triggered a split along the same lines as the one that had occurred during the 1970 break with the Stickies. It would have been another 'glorious defeat' for republicans to sing about as we faded into obscurity – and Adams was not about to sit back and let that happen. So he persevered with an armed struggle in which, in my opinion, he didn't really believe, in the hope that some unforeseen event would come along to transform the fortunes of the republican movement.

That unforeseen event came in the form of the 1981 hunger strike in the H-Blocks. Only after seeing the potential for a mass political movement during the hunger strike did Adams strike out and embrace electoral politics, and ultimately initiate the peace process. As more and more emphasis and money were put into the electoral development of Sinn Féin, Ivor Bell came to the conclusion that Adams's ultimate goal was to abandon the Armalite in favour of the ballot box. When Bell tried to reverse what he saw as the running down of the IRA, he was purged from the republican movement, under threat of execution, in 1985. It took thirteen years after the hunger strike, and a split in the IRA, before Adams felt confident enough to usher in the 1994 ceasefire – without the approval of rank-and-file IRA Volunteers.

While morale in H3 had lifted in the short term, there was still the problem of finding a way to bring the protest to a successful conclusion. The longer the protest went on, the closer we drew to a hunger strike. Already, while in H6, The Dark had lobbied the Army Council for permission to start a hunger strike. His request had been rejected on the grounds that not all the avenues that might bring about a settlement had been explored. As a result of his petition, the National H-Blocks and Armagh Committee was formed to mobilise support throughout Ireland on our behalf. (The women in Armagh Prison were also on protest for political status.) But I sensed that The Dark held out little hope that this would force the British government to give ground on the vital issues, and privately he told me that all that was happening was the postponement of the hunger strike. When he said the words 'hunger strike', he invariably pursed his lips and shrugged, because he knew that he would be leading it – a daunting prospect for any person.

8

By 1979, all wings had a tiny crystal radio, which each custodian kept secreted in his bum. These informed us of political developments outside. They were also useful for telling the time.

At the stroke of midnight, when 1979 vanished forever, the three blocks shouted over to each other, wishing their comrades a happy New Year. Then, in the stillness of the night, a voice could be heard singing, softly at first, then more loudly. I knew the owner of that voice to be Tommy Gorman: he was treating us to the most awe-inspiring rendition of 'The Foggy Dew' I had ever heard. Gorman had escaped from the *Maidstone* internment ship, moored at Belfast Lough, on 17 January 1972, with Jim Bryson, my legendary former OC in Ballymurphy, and Tommy 'Toddler' Tolan, a daredevil operator and a great pal of mine. Along with four others, Gorman, Bryson and Toddler had escaped by squeezing through the portholes to swim the half-mile to the far shore. (They had first covered themselves with butter to insulate themselves from the freezing water.) They then hijacked a bus and made good their escape.

How Bryson was able to squeeze through the tiny porthole was a mystery to me: he was a heavy-set man with huge shoulders and a belly that matched his physique. I had been interned on the *Maidstone* about seven weeks after that escape, and I remember thinking that I would have had difficulty getting through the porthole – and I was small in comparison to Bryson.

You could see why they wanted to escape from that horrible place, though. I arrived at the bottom of its gangplank amid a hailstorm, which was a refreshing relief from the claustrophobic atmosphere of the Holywood interrogation centre, on 16 February 1972. Two Peelers escorted me. Paras were guarding the ship at that time, and they had a sentry hut at the bottom of the gangplank. Two of them pleaded with the Peelers to be given five minutes with me, but thankfully their pleas were ignored and we proceeded up the gangplank. As I went on board, I couldn't help but remember a saying my father had: 'Show me the father and I'll show you the son.' Because of his involvement with the IRA, he had been interned aboard the *Al Rawdah*, a prison ship that had been anchored in Strangford Lough in 1940. Thirty-two years later, I found myself suffering the same fate.

I hated the *Maidstone*. It was an old World War II vessel that was completely unsuitable as a prison ship. We prisoners occupied the bottom two decks, while the top decks were given over to the Brit guards and the prison administration.

I stepped into the bowels of the ship to be greeted by my cousin Harryo, Rocky Morgan, with whom I had worked at the docks during my summer holidays from school, and many of my comrades from the 'Murph.

My first impression of the place was that it was a pit. I bedded down at the top of three folding bunks and tried to catch up on some sleep. That wasn't the easiest thing to do because there was a continuous, annoying hum, which I later found out was the heating system.

The Stickies occupied the very bottom deck, and we took the top tier. We had freedom of movement between the decks, and there was little friction between the two factions.

A small snooker table, a television and a table-tennis table provided the only recreation. From the first minute, the tedium and inactivity had me going up the walls. I showered two, sometimes three, times a day, not just because it was pleasant, but also because it passed the time. At other times, I would just lie on my bed, hoping to sleep for as long as possible; in sleep, there was hibernation from the dark winter that confronted our every waking minute. Table-tennis competitions and sing-songs helped to ease the boredom. I learned to play chess and that sometimes lifted the blues, but a 'dirty book' was by far the most pleasurable distraction of all.

The food was atrocious. The fry in the mornings was particularly vile, with rubbery sausages and eggs that floated on a sea of grease.

I remembered Toddler telling me that the seven men who had escaped had befriended a black seal by throwing it food so that it would swim in towards the ship. They did this to find out if there were any sensors in the water. The same black seal swam about the ship every day, looking for free food.

Weeks passed. The Stormont government was prorogued, but despite assurances from the authorities, nothing was done about conditions on the *Maidstone*. In late April, we threw our food out the portholes and went on hunger strike for better conditions. There were roughly one hundred and twenty of us on the protest; those with ulcers or who were in bad health weren't allowed to go on hunger strike. By the second day, there was nothing in my mind except food. The rubbery sausages didn't seem so rubbery now. After a week, the authorities capitulated, and we were all transferred to Long Kesh – after devouring a feed of rubbery sausages and spuds.

Tommy Gorman's melodic voice reached out and fired my spirit:

> The night fell black, and the rifle crack
> Made Perfidious Albion reel,
> Midst lead and rain, seven tongues of flame
> Shone out o'er the lines of steel.

> By each shining blade, a prayer was said,
> That to Ireland her sons be true,
> And when morning broke, still the war flag shook
> Its folds in The Foggy Dew.

As I lay on my bed, I marvelled at the words; surely a more evocative, patriotic song has never been penned. The 'seven tongues of flame' referred to in the song were the seven signatories of the 1916 Proclamation, who had been executed by the British for leading the rebellion. I remember thinking how wonderfully uplifting it would have been to be standing beside Pádraig Pearse as he spoke those beautiful words: 'We hereby proclaim the Irish Republic a Sovereign, Independent State . . .'

This journeying into romantic republicanism was common amongst the Blanketmen. The fact was that we existed in an idealistic time warp, wallowing in the vision of historical Irish heroes struggling for freedom. There was an almost biblical reverence for the 1916 Proclamation. Many of us could recite it by heart, and some had even taken the trouble to learn it in Irish. We justified all our actions and the entire struggle on the basis of the Proclamation – sometimes elevating the sacrifice of the signatories to a hallowed act.

The Gaelic culture that we nurtured and our emphasis on all things Irish rekindled the flame of resistance in us and inspired us to keep the faith. But it also inoculated us against the cruelty of our protest and the reality of our situation, and blinded us to the modern world and the political events of the day. Being denied access to the broad media, the only reports we got were gleaned from our radios: usually only the headline news of the day. This lack of first-hand political analysis meant that we had little idea of the dogmatic nature of the Thatcher government. Some time in the not-too-distant future, a number of blanketmen would again confront the British in hunger strikes. Would our romantic republicanism become their shroud?

Although Bobby Sands was a storyteller *par excellence*, Tommy McKearney from County Tyrone wasn't too far behind him. Tommy had a wonderful memory and the ability to make his stories come alive in the most vivid way. He was also the academic sort and was familiar with European history from the French Revolution to the present day. He gave us a nightly lecture for two weeks about Robespierre, Napoleon and Bismarck, the Iron Chancellor, among others. I was left wondering how he could remember all the characters and dates.

Debates in Irish were a feature of our entertainment and education programme. There were no sacred cows: anything could be discussed. During one debate about the way forward for the IRA, Tommy McKearney played devil's advocate and argued that the republican movement hadn't thought through the consequences of its campaign. In the event of the British withdrawing, he said, the loyalists would declare independence and we would be forced to take them on in open warfare.

Tommy went on to describe the nature of the loyalist forces that we would have to fight. He outlined the essential amenities that were exclusively under their control: the electricity service, the water supply, oil and petrol supplies and most of the food industry – almost all the ingredients for basic survival. Tommy argued that republican areas could be deprived of these essentials at a moment's notice and starved into submission without a shot being fired. Then he listed the tens of thousands of weapons the loyalists had at their disposal, compared to the meagre numbers the IRA possessed. His conclusion was that, in a civil war, we would be incapable of defending our people and would be annihilated.

Others disagreed, maintaining that revolutions are not always logical affairs. Sometimes the rebels started with only a handful of determined men against a mighty foe and succeeded against all the odds. The rebellions in Cuba, Vietnam, Nicaragua and even the United States were cited as examples of this. If the conditions for revolution existed – for example, if there was serious state oppression or an impoverished, subjugated population – and the revolutionaries offered a radical, attractive alternative to the regime, a successful revolution was possible. But did conditions for a successful revolution exist in the North? And if so, how would we go forward to victory? What military progress would we have to make to overcome the huge obstacles that stood in our way? It was a lively and sobering discussion.

I felt that Tommy had played devil's advocate too well, and it was a pensive young man who tried to close his eyes that night. Questions were forming in my mind: had the IRA leadership considered how this was all going to end? Were any serious considerations given to the enormous imbalance in the two opposing forces: the strength of the combined forces of the British government and militant loyalism versus the IRA? Was there a master plan to overcome such seemingly impossible odds? Was I taking McKearney's words too seriously? I felt I had good reason to do so. There seemed to be no easy answers, and there had been no deep analysis of the enemy's raw power; if even half of what Tommy McKearney had said were to come to pass, we would be in serious difficulties.

On another occasion, there was a discussion about how we were going to achieve power in the South as well as in the North. Even if we could prevail over the many obstructions that faced us in the North, other problems still confronted us. One big problem was that, in the South, the people tended to be conservative and not even remotely disposed towards mild socialism, never mind our 'blanket' brand of ultra-left politics.

We felt we had only two choices. We could either stage a *coup d'état*, overthrowing the Southern state by force and then creating a socialist republic, or build a strong political party and win power through the ballot box. A *coup d'état* was out of the question. We did not have the military strength to contemplate such a move, and even if such an undertaking were successful, the Irish people would probably resist us, and it was doubtful if the British government would tolerate an ultra-left state on their western flank.

To go down the ballot-box road was just as unpalatable. It would entail recognising Leinster House, the seat of the Irish Parliament, and taking our chances at the polls. Even if we could persuade IRA members and supporters to abandon their deeply held principles and recognise the Southern institutions, we would be destroyed at the polls because we had no political base worth talking about down south. Moreover, if such a base did exist, the Southern population, by and large, saw the war in the North as obscene and irrelevant. They wouldn't dream of voting for us. (Only after years of cessation, beginning in 1994, and relative peace was Sinn Féin able to build up a political base in the South.)

So we had a political Everest to climb in the North and a K2 to scale in the South. Was it any wonder that I questioned the direction of the war, if not its *raison d'être*? Foreboding and forbidden thoughts entered my head, and I found myself questioning the unquestionable: whether or not it was right to fight a war which seemed unwinnable. It was a notion that I didn't want to entertain at this stage, because the far-reaching consequences of this line of thinking left no room for manoeuvre or doubt. So I disappeared into that safe haven where all doubts were automatically put to bed: I put my faith in the leadership. Perhaps they had some super-plan for victory; I hoped so, though what it could be was beyond my comprehension. In the end, I felt I had no alternative but to exorcise those negative thoughts, because they were a challenge to my very soul as a republican.

McKearney's devil's advocacy led to some of us questioning the policy of abstentionism, of refusing to recognise the elected bodies that governed Ireland, North and South. We concluded that winning the war was all that mattered, and principles that blocked progress towards that goal were to be seen as self-defeating baggage that should be discarded as soon as possible. I felt that we should build a political party throughout Ireland; such a party had to be relevant to the Ireland of the late twentieth century – not a throwback to the civil-war politics of 1922. Its defining purpose would be to justify and advance the armed struggle. If that were achievable, our representatives could adequately act for their constituents on issues that mattered to them, such as the economy, planning and housing. By ostracising ourselves from those elected assemblies, we were, in my opinion, doing ourselves a great disservice.

Again, this thinking, while it may have been revolutionary in terms of republican thinking, was immature. To build that platform and transform our politics into something tangible, we were conveniently overlooking the fact that the people of Ireland had no time for the war in the North – indeed, they found it repugnant. Therefore there was little chance of them voting for us at the ballot box, even if we abandoned our abstentionist policy. So, to achieve a consequential presence in the partitionist institutions, we would have had to forswear the war. But the war was the be-all and end-all for us militant republicans. Constitutional politics was not a substitute for armed struggle; it was only ever a tactic – and an obnoxious one at that – which we barely tolerated. Our hearts told us that nothing but armed struggle would force the British to leave our country.

Socialism was the overwhelmingly dominant 'ism' in our wing. James Connolly, the executed 1916 socialist leader, asserted that it did not matter if the flag that flew over Dublin Castle was Irish or British. He believed that the capitalists would hijack the revolution unless the working class of Ireland owned and managed the means of production and the distribution of wealth. According to Connolly, the capitalists saw the working class only as an instrument to achieve their own greedy ends.

The former Cages men, in particular, were devout socialists, and Bobby Sands had gone on record as saying that he would not be interested in a united Ireland that wasn't socialist and that a capitalist Ireland wasn't worth the life of one Irishman. Many of us in the wing agreed with this, and we accepted that socialism was more important than nationalism, even though we saw both as part of Ireland's future. Socialism represented a greed-free society where everyone was motivated by communal benevolence and where reward for talent was measured, not in personal gain or a big bank balance, but in the opportunity to bring benefits to society as a whole. It was the perfect society for imperfect and weak human beings.

Tommy McKearney's vision of a socialist Ireland was an extreme one, and it found little favour with most of the lads in the wing. He expounded the view that what was needed was a totalitarian system that excluded dissenting opinion or capitalist political parties which threatened the revolution and the socialist way of life. At the time I areed with the logic of McKearney's position. There was uproar amongst the farmers in our midst when he advocated the collectivisation of farms.

While McKearney's socialist republic tasted more than a little bitter to some, I thought it illustrated the enormity of the task ahead of us if we wanted to convert the Irish people to socialism. How could we bring the nation along with us on the socialist road if we could not even convert some of our own Volunteers to the idea of the state ownership of land?

McKearney's socialist vision aside, the dream of a new and fairer system did not go away, and the idea of freedom from greed and selfishness sustained the protest every bit as much as the struggle for political status. There was something of the crusader about us, a sense that we were the enlightened ones who knew there was a better, more Christian way. Socialism was akin to Christianity for many of us, with its central tenets of justice and equality. Jesus Christ, we believed, had been the first socialist.

Perhaps the most crucial element of our socialist thinking was that, for a while, we found utopia in the only place it resides on this earth – within ourselves. The vision was enough, the ethos self-sustaining; the practicalities and nuances were a matter for another time and place.

9

On 17 January 1980, the sad news reached us that Kevin 'Dee' Delaney, a member of the Ballymurphy staff of 1972, had been killed after being blown up by his own bomb on a train outside Lisburn, County Antrim. Also blown up, although he survived, was a fellow Volunteer, 'Jokey' Flynn. (Jokey eventually ended up as my cellmate in Long Kesh.) The Dark knew Dee from the Cages, where he had been sentenced to ten years for possession, and he remarked, 'That man knew what he was dyin' for,' meaning that Dee was a convinced socialist.

I knew a different Dee. He and I had billeted in the same houses in New Barnsley and Ballymurphy in the winter of 1971 (when we were both kids on the run), and we had knocked about together during those dark nights. A lady who lived in New Barnsley Park had put us up one night. She had a huge double bed with fresh white sheets. I remember Dee's delight at having such luxury (he had been on the run longer than me and had spent a lot of his time sleeping on sofas). Although the British were raiding his house regularly, he would insist that we nipped into his mother's house at the bottom of Ballymurphy Parade for a cup of tea and a bite to eat.

Mrs Delaney, while delighted to see him, would always usher us out as soon as the meal was over.

I thought that, by this time, I would have been insulated from the pain of comrades dying, but it never got any better. The Dark and I then had a conversation about Dee and those who had died in Ballymurphy since 1971.

As usual, The Dark was a mine of information. He told me that, before the 1972 truce, he had been sent up to Ballymurphy to speak to Jim Bryson, who, after escaping from the *Maidstone* prison ship, had returned to take command of the Ballymurphy IRA. I asked The Dark why it was thought necessary to speak to Bryson; he told me that some members of the Brigade staff thought that Bryson was 'too free a spirit' and that he might ignore the order to stop operations and so torpedo the Truce. When The Dark put it like that, the pieces began to fall into place. I knew Bryson well because I used to meet him almost every day; he was the type of man who had an inbuilt distrust of men who had never stood in the gap of danger or fired a shot for Ireland. (Bryson had never been found wanting when it came to walking that particular tightrope, and he was usually at the forefront of operations.) To him, the lowly Volunteer who sat with a rifle for hours or days at a window or in a hedge, waiting for a target, was worthy of more respect than a dozen armchair generals who gave orders from afar.

The leadership would have been right to be suspicious of Bryson's independent demeanour, and his undoubted belligerence at any hint of compromise would have marked him down as a possible loose cannon. On top of that, Bryson ran a very successful IRA company, whose kill-rate in Belfast was second to none, and he would have been reluctant to call his men off when they had the British on the ropes. (In Ballymurphy, the King's Own Regiment, a novice regiment, was having a difficult time at the hands of Bryson's men.)

At the time of the proposed truce, The Dark was on the Belfast Brigade staff, but we all recognised that he had risen to his position of prominence within the IRA because of his organisational skills. He was a leading force in one of the most successful IRA units in Belfast – the 'D' (for 'Dogs') unit in the Lower Falls – a unit with a prolific record for killing British soldiers. As such, he was one of the few leaders for whom Bryson had respect. The Dark told me that he had met Jim in our company headquarters, in an upstairs flat in the Bullring. Spread out against a wall were two dozen rifles and sub-machine-guns. As a result of that meeting, The Dark moved Bryson from a position of outright hostility to acceptance of the ceasefire.

The Dark asked me how I had first heard of the Truce. I told him that Bryson had called a Company Council meeting in Whitecliffe Parade in Ballymurphy, days before it came into effect. Besides the Company staff, our former Company OC and our then Battalion OC, Pat McClure, was in attendance. It was Pat who broke the news that a truce was imminent. Of the dozen or so men who had attended that historic meeting, Jim Bryson, Tommy 'Toddler' Tolan, Paddy Mulvenna, John Stone and Dee Delaney had since been killed as a result of the war. Gerry Kelly, who had also been there, was doing life in England for the Old Bailey bombings, and most of the few of us who were still alive were in the H-Blocks or the Cages.

The ceasefire broke in Lenadoon, an estate in Andersonstown, two weeks after it was called. Ironically, Bryson and Toddler fired the first volley of shots from a Lewis machine-gun, signalling a restart to the war. (Jim

Bryson was shot dead by British soldiers in Ballymurphy in August 1973 after friction with the Stickies; Toddler was shot dead by the Stickies in July 1977.)

Secret talks to resolve the blanket protest had been going on for almost a year between Cardinal Ó Fiaich, the Catholic Primate of Ireland, and the British, but nothing of substance had come out of them. The Cardinal had had discussions with senior republicans, who told him bluntly that if the talks failed the prisoners would go on hunger strike. He dutifully relayed this to the British.

As the talks stumbled on, it became obvious that the British government sensed that the protest was running out of steam. More and more republican prisoners were conforming to the prison regime directly after being sentenced (as opposed to going on the blanket), and the number on the protest – around three hundred – wasn't rising. At every opportunity, the British were quick to point out this inequality in the number-count. They claimed that eight hundred prisoners, republican and loyalist, were accepting prison rules and that only a rump of diehards was bucking the system. Soon there would be more republican prisoners wearing the prison gear than there were on the protest, and that was a dangerous psychological situation for us to be in. The 'three hundred Spartans' were beginning to feel isolated, and the prospect of a hunger strike was moving closer all the time.

I felt The Dark's growing impatience with the stagnant situation and the apparent failure of the Ó Fiaich initiative. He told me that he had pencilled in a provisional date in the middle of the summer for the hunger strike to begin and had sent a comm (communiqué) to the IRA Army Council seeking permission to begin the strike.

Gerry Adams was a personal friend of The Dark's. They had been arrested together, along with Ivor Bell, in 1972 and had remained confidants while imprisoned in the Cages. The Dark lionized Adams whenever the opportunity arose. Adams was also recognised as the leading strategist in the republican movement. Adams had received the Army Council's reply to The Dark's request to start a hunger strike and communicated it to him. The Army Council did not want a hunger strike. They did not believe it would succeed. Adams gave his friend his personal opinion. Margaret Thatcher, the British prime minister, would definitely let men die. He knew that The Dark would be leading the hunger strike, and he told him bluntly that, if he continued to pursue this course of action, he would be dead within months. He went on to make a personal appeal, as one friend to another, for The Dark to think again. Personal friendship aside, nothing was going to change The Dark's view, but another development arose that was to put the hunger strike plan on hold.

Martin Meehan was one of the most prominent republicans in Belfast. He had been the OC of the Third Battalion, which covered the north and east of the city, and had acquired a reputation as a fearless leader. In March 1980, he was sentenced to twelve years for kidnapping eighteen-year-old Stephen McWilliams, a suspected informer. After being convicted, Meehan told the judge: 'You know, and God knows, and I know, I was not involved in this.'

In late April 1980, a frustrated Meehan went on hunger strike to protest his innocence. The Dark was livid at this unforeseen turn of events because it put his timeframe for a summer hunger strike on hold. (There was no way we could have two hunger strikes for different reasons in the H-Blocks.) Not only that, but were the republican movement to rally behind Meehan and initiate street protests (which didn't happen), it could subvert the larger strike when it eventually came: mobilising people in mass protests in time leads to frustration and weariness, and those emotions could translate into an apathetic response to the hunger strike for political status. Consequently, The Dark wrote to the Army Council asking its members to order Meehan off his hunger strike. Whether or not Meehan received the order is unclear, but he remained on hunger strike for sixty-six days, and even went on thirst strike for the last four days. (Meehan was a bull of a man.) Only a personal plea from Cardinal Ó Fiaich, with a promise that he would take up his case, persuaded Meehan to call off his strike.

Meehan actually did us a favour, although he didn't know it. While there is no good time to go on hunger strike, summer is probably the worst season of all, because people have too many other distractions at that time of year – holidays in particular. As a result of the Meehan hunger strike, The Dark postponed the summer hunger strike and decided to go for the autumn.

Some writers wax lyrical about autumn and of how the leaves dance a lively jig in the swirling wind. I didn't see it like that. I have always equated autumn with death. The leaves may have caught an imaginative eye as they spun about in the wind, but the reality was that their life's journey was nearly at an end. Now I had another reason to loathe that particular season.

10

I was shifted out of The Dark's cell and into a cell with Colm Scullion from Bellaghy, County Derry, about March 1980. Two of Scull's toes had been amputated after he was blown up by his own car bomb in Ballymena.

A livelier soul than Scull didn't exist. I had difficulty understanding him at first because he spoke a dialect that was indigenous to his native Bellaghy; it was so unintelligible that I called it 'Bellawegian'. I had to battle with the difference between a 'wee lock' and a 'brave lock' to describe quantity. He called girls 'blades' or 'cutties'; Scull told me that these words went right back to the court of Elizabeth I. Scull had a Gold Fáinne in Bellawegian.

I found him a fascinating character who loved history and valued his country life. He told tales of 'poochin" (poaching) salmon and eels in the dead of night from the River Bann and of being left in a bed of reeds when he was a nipper at the side of the river, while his father netted the fish.

Joe O'Boyle was a Lough Neagh fisherman who lived in the village of Toome, County Antrim. He hated poachers. One night, we were standing at the cell windows staring out at a dark, cloudless sky, and Joe began to tell us that it was on a night like this, at 'the dark of the moon', that the silver eels, the main catch in the lough, began their yearly migration from Lough Neagh to the Sargasso Sea in the North Atlantic (between the West Indies and the Azores). What the signal was for the mobilisation, or how they all knew that their time had come to move on, was a mystery. Nonetheless, it was at that juncture that they left for the Sargasso Sea, where they spawned and died. Then the cycle of life turned once more as their elvers made the three-thousand-mile journey back across the Atlantic to Lough Neagh; on the night of the eel-run, they would follow in the stream of their parents and also strike out towards the Atlantic.

This migration gave the Lough Neagh fishermen their harvest: they would catch thousands of eels at their fishing weir at Toome. Joe explained that the weir extended across two-thirds of the Bann and that the other third was left to ensure that enough fish escaped to spawn in the Sargasso Sea in order to secure the next year's harvest.

Scull, ever the imp, reminded Joe that those eels that escaped the cull had to get past Lough Beg, in Ballyscullion, and that it was his duty to enforce the Clan Scullion's ancient right to confiscate a 'pan or two of eels'. Joe retorted indignantly that Scull was 'a no-toed, backwoods poacher'. Scull reminded Joe that his licence to fish had been granted by King James I, who had sequestered it, by force of arms, from his ancestor Feargus Ó Scullion, the local chieftain.

Scull really didn't regard poaching as stealing. He told me that his ancestors had been the owners of the land before the plantation of Ulster by Scottish Protestants and English adventurers in the seventeenth century and that the Planters had forced his ancestors into bog land at the side of the Bann. The townland he lived in was called, appropriately, Ballyscullion. The eels, as far as he was concerned, were rightly his in the first place.

In many ways, Scull was the epitome of the aggrieved and dispossessed countryman. He could trace his ancestors back to 1306; as lords in their own lands, they had the fishing rights for Lough Beg (granted by the O' Neills of Tyrone, Kings of Ulster), an extension of the much larger Lough Neagh. Foreign conquest and the plantation of Ulster had annulled those rights in the eyes of his enemies, but not for Scull (who still thinks he owns Loch Beg). I saw in him the anger of one who wanted to right an ancient wrong.

The story of Arthur Chichester was another of Scull's favourite topics. Chichester was a seventeenth-century English highwayman who was credited with the found-ing of Belfast, but Scull recalled stories, handed down from his forebears, which told of how Chichester, in his quest to eradicate the native Irish, had burnt every cabin in his path along the Lough Neagh shore and put men, women and children to the fire and sword, 'leaving nothing but the ravens alive'. I got the distinct impression that, in Scull's consciousness, these events had not happened three hundred years ago, but rather yesterday. Countrymen have long memories.

After being in the cell with Scull for a while, I began to acquire an understanding of the temperaments of those comrades who live in small rural communities. They were parochial – their isolated upbringing made that understandable – but they had a great appreciation of nature and history and were much more at peace with themselves than us city and town boys.

Scull was also a very jovial character and abided rigidly by three rules:

1. Never do today what you can do tomorrow.
2. Always get the biggest plate of food as it comes in the door.
3. 'Clean mate [meat] never fattened a sow.'

The first two were self-explanatory, but 'Clean mate never fattened a sow'? He told me that this meant that we shouldn't be too fussy about the quality of food offered to us; it was all there was, and there was no point in not eating it. Scull ate it all right; he would have eaten dog-food if that was what was on the plate.

One night, Tommy McKearney gave us a lecture on the history of the IRA since the 1921 Anglo-Irish Treaty. One of the salient points of his lecture was that involvement in the republican movement was usually hereditary – that is, certain families had produced IRA Volunteers from the Treaty era until the present day.

To prove his point, he decided to do a census in the wing. Right enough, almost everyone could trace a degree of ancestral involvement with the IRA, although some connections were a bit tenuous. When it came to our cell, I told Tommy of my father's involvement in the forties and fifties IRA campaign. When it was Scull's turn, he said that his grandfather had been in jail in the twenties for 'possession'. Later on that night, a curious McKearney called Scull up to the cell door and asked him what his grandfather had been caught with. Undaunted, Scull replied that he had been caught with a poteen-still and had been sentenced to six months. McKearney roared with laughter, as Scull went on to say that his grandfather was a political prisoner because his poteen-production business had been undermining the British economy.

In the cell next to us were Tom 'Buck' Bradley from Ardoyne and Aidan Slane from Tyrone. If ever there was a mismatch, these two boys were it: Tom Buck was a rough-talking city slicker, unlike Aidan, who was a farmer.

Scull took great pleasure in torturing Aidan. On one occasion, he branded Aidan 'the political correspondent for the *Beano*', the children's comic – meaning that Aidan hadn't the wit to rise above comic-book politics. The blanket protest wasn't a place for the easily offended.

Scull and Aidan loved the poetry of Seamus Heaney and used to discuss particular poems out the cell windows. The rascality arose in me one morning, and I decided to compose a piece of gibberish and present it to Aidan to see what his response would be:

A dark dearth of unbecoming solace,
Penetrated the grey mosaic of demented light,
As a flock of blue robin redbreasts hovered overhead.

Aidan was given the poem through the pipes and, after reading it, said, 'Sufferin' Jaysus, O' Rawe, that's heavy!'

I knew he was bursting to laugh, but I kept serious. 'Did you get the gist of it, Aidan?'

'I'm not sure. I didn't know there was such a thing as "blue robin redbreasts".'

'It's symbolic, Aidan. They're blue 'cause they're sad, just like us. Yet they're the most beautiful of birds.'

Scull, who was having difficulty suppressing his laughter, chirped in, saying that the robin redbreast probably flew from south Derry into Tyrone, and the

Tyrone men were such 'a bunch of hungry whores' that it was blue from starvation.

Aidan was more than up to Scull's provocation, and he commented that the 'bogmen of south Derry' would know a lot about hunger, having surrendered their prime land to 'the Sassenach'.

After a bit of banter between them, Aidan got back to the poem. 'It's a sad poem, all right.' He waited for a minute before saying: 'Jaysus, Ricky, I didn't think you were that sad!'

That was it. Scull couldn't hold it any longer and erupted, followed by Aidan and myself,

'Oh my God! I'll tell you what, O' Rawe, I thought there for a minute you were losin' it altogether. "Blue robin redbreasts"!'

One day a screw we called 'Fly-Catcher Lip' (because he had a very prominent upper lip) was patrolling the yard. He had just called us 'Fenian bastards' when Scull, shouting through the cell window, asked him which of his mates was screwing his wife when he was at work. The eejit took the bait, squealing that he would kill the person who had just said that and that the culprit hadn't the balls to identify himself. Scull then shouted out that his name was Hector McNeill and that he would kick his bollocks in if he ever came near his door.

Poor Hector had been enjoying the craic up until then and had already asked Jimmy Teapot where Scull had got the bottle from, but when he heard his name mentioned and realised that he was likely to take the hit, he panicked and jumped up to the window, shouting to Fly-Catcher Lip that he was Hector McNeill, and he wasn't the person shouting, but that it was Colm Scullion. Hector finished off by promising Scull the hiding of his life.

Sometimes the hilarity was fabulous on the blanket.

There was a wealth of humour, cultural diversity and expression that I found uplifting. Despite the hardship of prison life, I had many tremendous experiences with Bobby, Bik, The Dark, McKearney, Scull, Aidan, Tom Buck, Teapot, Hector, Dollhead and the rest of the lads. It was a life which carried with it many of the horrors of the concentration camps, but which was also lightened at times with side-splitting banter.

11

By the end of the summer of 1980, it was obvious that the British government had no intention of bringing about the conditions that would end the protest. Against the backdrop of a hunger strike, Cardinal Ó Fiaich issued a statement in September saying that the talks with the Northern Ireland Office had not broken down and that, if the prison uniform was abolished and a more liberal, educational regime put in place for all prisoners, then, he felt certain, the protest would end.

But still the British doggedly refused to consider any form of compromise. They countered Ó Fiaich's statement with a breathtakingly arrogant response that stated they wouldn't discuss or negotiate the principle of political or special-category status. They went on to echo Margaret Thatcher's words: 'Murder is murder, is murder, is murder.'

Bobby Sands had a 'Mrs Dale', our name for the small crystal radios we had smuggled in. He had been listening closely to the government statement while waiting to be called for a visit. After that, and having put 'Mrs Dale' safely back in storage, he went to Cell 26 to get ready for the visit. Ralphie Gilmore, the Class Officer, was there on his own. Bobby asked him what he thought of the statement. Ralphie replied that it was very strong. Bobby asked him if the British had said 'Murder is murder, is murder, is murder.' Ralphie said that, funnily enough, they had. Bobby then went on to quote almost directly from the statement, winking and smiling at Ralphie at the same time. Ralphie's mouth opened wide. In the end he asked Bobby if the deal was done. Bobby smiled again and told Ralphie that he shouldn't trust the British. Bobby could be a rascal when he wanted to be.

Through sharing a cell with The Dark for six months, I had come to respect his opinion, and he mine. He made me aware at Mass one Sunday that, despite what the 'Big Lad' (Gerry Adams) had said, a hunger strike was the sole option left open for us to bring the protest to a conclusion. The talks had only delayed the final round in this epic battle of wills; the curtain had come down on reason and compromise.

I was completely against a hunger strike. As I had foreseen on my journey up to H3, and had told Blute that first night on the blanket, I suspected that the protest would eventually come to this, and I felt certain too that the British government had factored it into its calcul-ations and was probably spoiling for the confrontation. The Thatcher government had spurned every chance to end the stalemate honourably and was ready, I thought, for a hunger strike. For us Blanketmen, the lack of any other remedy forced us to face our own Stalingrad – and the enemy was at the gate.

From that moment on, I saw The Dark in a different light. He was going to lead the hunger strike, and I couldn't help but feel that his time on this earth was drawing to a close. I could see that he was fortifying himself for the coming battle; an aura of pathos seemed to emanate from deep within him. My friend, my comrade, was on the verge of giving his life for us.

To maximise the number of men on protest, the prison leadership of The Dark and Bobby Sands decided to send a man up to the conforming blocks to persuade those republicans that were 'wearing the gear' to join us on protest at the start of the hunger strike. The man selected to perform this task was Seán 'Glas' Chillingworth.

Seán Glas had been sentenced to twenty years for the attempted murder of British soldiers after he was wounded during a car chase in the Andersonstown area of west Belfast on 10 August 1976. It was said at the time that his pursuers had fired about sixty shots at the car. The driver of the car, Volunteer Danny Lennon, was shot dead at the wheel during the car chase and, as a result, the car mounted the kerb and ploughed out of control into the railings of Saint John the Baptist School on Finaghy Road North. Tragically, Anne Maguire was wheeling her six-week-old son, Andrew, in a pram past the school at the time. Alongside her was her eight-year-old daughter, Joanne, who was riding a bike, and her son, John, who was two years old. The Maguires took the full force of the impact. Joanne and Andrew died instantly, and John died later that day in hospital. Anne Maguire was critically injured but finally recovered, only to take her own life on 12 January 1980.

The deaths of the Maguire children touched everyone. I remember my own sense of devastation at this poor family's grief. Their deaths gave birth to the Peace People movement in 1976. This movement was led by Anne Maguire's sister Mairead Corrigan, her neighbour Betty Williams and journalist Ciarán McKeown. The Peace People was able to take advantage of the mood of war-weariness that existed within both sections of the community, and mobilised thousands of people behind one demand: no more killing. The campaign eventually faltered and lost ground in the nationalist areas. In due course it fizzled out.

Seán Glas was the perfect choice to speak to the other republican prisoners. He did not mince his words and had a persuasive ability to convince doubters that duty called and that what was needed was to show a united republican front.

A bitter wind was blowing down from the Arctic Circle into the North. I felt its icy sting as it entered my cell. Or was I shaking because of what Tommy McKearney had said to us as he prepared to begin his fast, that he wanted to be buried in Mayo along with his grandfather? Perhaps it was his reference to the Spartan mothers who had told their sons, when they were preparing to go into battle with the Persians, that they had to come home either with their shields or upon them.

On 27 October 1980, seven of our comrades embarked on hunger strike to obtain five demands, which encapsulated our right to be recognised as political prisoners. These were:

1. The right not to have to wear prison uniform.
2. The right not to have to do prison work.
3. The right to have free association among ourselves.
4. The right to receive a weekly parcel, a weekly visit and unlimited letters.

5. The return of all remission lost as a result of
   the protest.

Those on hunger strike were Brendan 'The Dark' Hughes, Tom McFeely, Tommy McKearney, Leo Greene, Raymond McCartney, Seán McKenna and John Nixon, the OC of the Irish National Liberation Army prisoners. Seven men were selected out of many Volunteers because seven men had signed the sacred Proclamation of 1916. It was hoped that the analogy of sacrifice would be recognised and act as a catalyst to muster the Irish people to our cause.

The timing was important. It was estimated that the critical phase of the hunger strike, when the first death would be likely to occur, would coincide with the Christmas period, the season of goodwill. While the woman who lived in 10 Downing Street may have been disinclined to extend goodwill to the hunger strikers, it was nonetheless reckoned that she would be extremely uncomfortable if a striker was to die on, say, Christmas Day. All six counties in the occupied North had a prisoner represented on the strike to maximize public opinion and put as much pressure as possible on the British government.

Tommy McKearney's cell door opened and I heard him quietly tell Ralphie Gilmore, the screw in charge of the wing, that he was on hunger strike for political status. It was said without emotion, and Ralphie showed no emotion. It was as if he was expecting no less. A moment later, the door was closed. The breakfast of cornflakes and milk didn't appeal to either Scull or myself, so we threw it on the pile in the corner.

On the day the hunger strike started, two hundred former conforming prisoners joined the protest, thanks to Seán Glas. Vanload after vanload pulled up into the yard of H3, and that was a great comfort. It raised morale: for the first time in a long while we could claim that most republican prisoners in the H-Blocks were behind us. We welcomed the '*émigrés*' as comrades and fellow republicans and tried to make them feel at home. At the back of our minds, though, was the realisation that if things didn't turn out as we hoped, these men would probably abandon us as quickly as they had embraced us. We all knew that their mind-set was different from ours. (There were exceptions to the rule, as it turned out, however, and quite a few of the '*émigrés*' stayed solid throughout both hunger strikes.)

Bobby Sands had taken over from The Dark as the Block OC, and Bik became public-relations officer of the prisoners. Our propaganda campaign was greatly intensified, and we worked night and day to influence public opinion in support of our five demands.

Almost immediately, the campaign outside the prison took off. Thousands of people were on the march in Belfast, Dungannon, Derry, Dublin and other places throughout the country. Abroad, the campaign was generating huge support and interest, and television crews from around the world rushed to Belfast to cover the story.

The Dark and Tommy seemed to be in fine spirits, although I suspected that deep down they must have been dejected about the predicament in which they found themselves. I tried to imagine their lonely journey into the unknown: the inner knowledge that it would all be over within weeks and that, with their life-force ebbing away, every moment was now precious. I saw the sorrow in The Dark's eyes and his kindly, paternal half-grin that tried to, but couldn't, disguise the wretchedness of his situation. And still their captors sneered as they left food in their cells at mealtimes.

The British had decided against the policy of force-feeding the hunger strikers, a policy they had pursued against Dolores and Marion Price, Gerry Kelly and Hugh Feeney when they had gone on hunger strike for repatriation in 1974 after being convicted for the Old Bailey bombings. Another republican, Michael Gaughan, had died on 3 June 1975 after being force-fed while on hunger strike in Parkhurst Prison on the Isle of Wight.

Every day, the strikers had their weight, blood pressure and temperature taken by medical staff. Prisoners who had visits then relayed these details to the IRA leadership outside. Our outside leadership told the strikers that it was important that they drink at least eight pints of water a day to keep up their strength.

The weeks ran on, and the hunger strikers were moved to the prison hospital. On 3 December, three female republican prisoners from Armagh Jail, Mairéad Farrell, Mary Doyle and Mairéad Nugent, joined the hunger strike. That had a dramatic effect on us, because somehow the opinion gained ground that one, or possibly all three, of the women might reach the danger point of the hunger strike before their male counterparts. But there wasn't much we could do: they were strong-willed and determined to play their part in the hunger strike. In mid-December, another thirty men went on the strike to show that we had the stamina to see the protest through to the end.

All sorts of manoeuvrings seemed to be under way behind the scenes. Northern Ireland Office officials were visiting the strikers, and I got the impression, for the first time, that a solution might be in the air.

Cardinal Ó Fiaich and others were conveying the impression that the clothes issue could be resolved. If that was the case, then I thought a dilemma was facing the leadership. Would they end the hunger strike there and then, on the basis that being allowed to wear our own clothes would be enough? Or would more concessions become available under the table as the strike progressed and pressure mounted on the British? Was this the final opportunity to end the strike and save the lives of the hunger strikers?

I brought to Bobby and Bik's attention my view that the British could be looking for a way out with a minimum loss of face, and if the rumoured concessions on clothes were true, Bobby and Bik needed to consider a response to clarify the situation and get a statement ready. I emphasised the word 'clarify' because I didn't want to influence any decision they made. Since I was not directly involved with the leadership and was not party to its strategic considerations, I had no idea what the minimum requirements were that would bring about an end to the strike. I did not even know how the five demands had been formulated or what the fine details were. The outside leadership drafted them, and there was little or no input from the average Blanketman. Revolutionary armies, by their nature, are not democratic institutions, and the IRA was and is no different.

In my heart, though, I felt there was a danger of overestimating and perhaps fatally overplaying the limited power that was at our disposal. Public demonstrations and shows of strength on the outside meant little to a strong government which had a record of ignoring popular protest. To my mind, we needed to focus on the possible and resist the lure of the improbable. At all times, I bore in mind that this was a life-and-death struggle and that it was our comrades' lives that were at stake.

Still, Bobby didn't think that such a statement was necessary and gave me a polite 'no thanks' for my contribution. The next day a comm came in from the outside leadership, echoing my views on the matter. Bobby was told to issue a statement, and Bik drafted it, saying that a satisfactory solution to the clothes issue alone would not bring about an end to the hunger strike. Inadvertently, and without knowing it, I had propelled myself into a position of future leadership. The results still haunt me twenty-four years later.

Bobby and Bik continually spoke in code, but it didn't take a genius to work out that they were in contact with John Hume, the SDLP leader, Charlie Haughey, the Irish Taoiseach, and, most importantly, the British government. A Redemptorist priest from Clonard Monastery in Belfast, Father Brendan Meagher, codenamed 'The Angel', liaised with the British government's go-between, Michael Oatley, a member of the British Secret Intelligence Service, MI6. (Someone in the chain of contact had the touch of the dramatist about them, because Oatley was given the codename 'The Mountain Climber': an appropriate pseudonym, given the task that lay ahead of him.) Danny Morrison, codenamed 'Pennies from Heaven', was our immediate contact from the republican movement. I assumed that, if I was right, they could only be negotiating a settlement. I dearly hoped they were.

By 18 December, the hunger strikers had not eaten for over seven weeks. Bobby was summoned to the camp hospital about ten o'clock that night. (We later found out that, while there, he had met Father Meagher, who presented him with a document from the British government on prison procedures.) You could feel the tension on the wing as Bobby got ready to leave for the hospital. Everyone knew that this was an important meeting, because reports had been circulating that Seán McKenna was in a critical condition. After an hour and a half, Bobby returned with the news that the hunger strike was over. My immediate reaction was one of huge relief, but this was tempered when Bobby said: '*Ní fhuaireamar faic.*' ('We didn't get anything.')

I was shell-shocked. What had happened to make The Dark end the hunger strike without a solution? I crept into bed, trying to make sense of it. Was there something Bobby wasn't telling us? Had the British government insisted on the strike ending before they would make concessions? Was this part of a clandestine deal? The words '*Ní fhuaireamar faic*' echoed in my ears. I came to the conclusion that Bobby was telling us that the hunger strike had collapsed.

Bobby let the other Blocks know about the bad news. When he returned, he reported that Father Meagher had told The Dark that a statement from the British government, allegedly containing a deal, had been in transit from Aldergrove Airport, Belfast. The crux of the matter was that before the message could reach The Dark, Seán McKenna would be dead. So The Dark intervened to save Seán's life and ended the hunger strike, on the understanding that what was in the document contained the nucleus of a settlement.

In fact, though none of us realised this at the time, the hunger-strike strategy had been fatally flawed from the start. The seven men had embarked on it in the knowledge that they would probably die; in many ways, that insulated them from having to face a cruel reality that might confront them down the road. They accepted our negotiating arrangement of Gerry Adams and Danny Morrison from the republican leadership, and Bobby Sands, the OC of the prisoners, being present in the event of the British coming to them with a potential settlement. While this sounded like a prudent safeguard against the possibility of starving and dying men accepting a less-than-satisfactory deal, it conveniently overlooked some odious possibilities that none of us envisaged at the time.

Our staff and the hunger strikers accepted that, should the British wish to settle, it would be on the most favourable terms for themselves and at a time when the first hunger striker was on the brink of death. What if the British came along with the bones of the five demands, but also with the proviso that Adams and Morrison would not be allowed into the jail to ratify them? In that event, should the hunger strikers stick rigidly to the negotiating arrangement and let their comrade die? Even if the British gave in to the demand for Adams and Morrison to be present, what if the first hunger striker died while they were *en route* from Belfast? We had to bear in mind that no one knew exactly how long a hunger striker had left from the time he went into a coma until he died. And if the two men made it to the jail, how long would it take them to study and pass judgment on the nuances of any proposals? The biggest 'what if' of all was that, if Adams and Morrison had got into the prison and subsequently decided to reject the proposals, their negative response would have resulted in a hunger striker dying – a politically catastrophic result.

The flaw was not, as some observers believe, that The

Dark was wrong to intervene to save Seán McKenna's life on the back of a vague set of proposals that he hadn't been given the chance to consider; the flaw was in the seven-man hunger-strike tactic itself – alongside a disastrously ill-thought-out negotiating strategy. Both were inherently self-defeating.

I don't know exactly what transpired in the prison hospital before Bobby Sands's arrival, or the precise reason why The Dark and four of his comrades decided to abandon the fast. (Tommy McKearney was going into the first stages of a coma when the strike ended and was delirious, so he never contributed to their decision.) Nonetheless, at that moment my heart went out to The Dark as I considered the pressure he must have been under. To accept that a deal was on the way and take the British at their word, or to let a comrade die – never had a republican been placed in such a dilemma.

As it turned out, the 'deal' *en route* from London was little more than a reiteration of the prison rules that had existed for hundreds of years. Our suspicion was that the British had switched documents the moment they heard the strike was over. I didn't know what was supposed to be in the document – or if there had been a switch. The only undisputed fact is that a document existed.

The hunger strike was over. Where to now?

12

'Liam Óg', one of our main contacts in the outside leadership during the hunger strike, sent a comm in to Bobby on 20 December 1980 saying that he never wanted to go through a day like that (19 December) in his life again. His meaning was obvious: it had been a mammoth task to cover up the fact that the hunger strike had collapsed and that the five demands were as far from being met as ever.

To keep up the illusion that we had gained something from the hunger strike, Bobby and Bik told us to put on an air of elation during visits with our families. I remember having a visit with Bernie on the morning of 20 December and telling her that a durable deal had been worked out and that it wouldn't be long before we were off the protest and in our own civilian clothes. Inside, though, I was gutted. This subterfuge was thought necessary because the collapse of the hunger strike had dealt a heavy blow to the struggle and our support base needed reassurance that the hunger strikers hadn't just called the thing off rather than die for their beliefs. (As I explained earlier, it wasn't as simple as that, but we were dealing with our supporters, and they saw things in black and white.)

That afternoon the wing was quiet, even solemn: the realisation that nothing had been achieved hit home cruelly. Our last and most valuable card had been played – and had proved to be woefully unsuccessful. There was nothing left at our disposal to influence change. We were all shattered, as the prospect of perennial protest loomed ghost-like before us. On a more positive note, Seán McKenna had been snatched from the jaws of death, and his six comrades in the hospital wing were slowly recovering from their ordeal.

Already, many of the two hundred republican prisoners who had been conforming to prison rules but had joined our protest when the hunger strike started had abandoned ship and once again embraced the prison regime. Bobby had been trying to hold back as many of them as possible with promises of a fresh approach to the situation, but the truth was that there was nothing left in the tank and, as a result, the holding exercise could not last long. When the *émigrés* did an about-turn, there would once again be more conforming republican prisoners than protesters. There was no avenue left to secure a resolution of the protest, and morale had plummeted to depths we had never imagined possible.

As usual, Bobby Sands radiated hope and was closely studying the document that The Dark had been told would be enough to end the protest to see if he could navigate a way out of our depressing predicament. From his demeanour and remarks, I knew there was no comfort in it, and eventually he concluded that it was 'full of holes' and open to any interpretation the British government wanted to put on it. They certainly weren't going to be favourably disposed towards our wishful translation of its contents.

Bobby called Bik, Jake Jackson, Pat Mullin and myself

to our doors to discuss future strategy. If the British had had the services of a *Gaeilgeoir*, an Irish speaker, they would have had an eagle's-eye view of where we were and where we would be going. I had nothing much to say; nobody had. We spent some time discussing the possible abandonment of the protest, and going into the mainstream prison system with the intention of wrecking it. We concluded that, while we could destroy the prison workshops quite easily through acts of sabotage and through the sheer strength of our numbers and command structure, we would have to wear the gear, and that would defeat the whole point of being on the blanket in the first place. This realisation reinforced the argument for accepting the clothes initiative that Cardinal Ó Fiaich had been pushing for both before and during the hunger strike. If that initiative had been available to us at the time of our discussion, we would have jumped at it and ended the protest there and then. Alas, the victor wanted to claim the spoils.

The discussion seemed to be going nowhere, and there was deadly silence when Pat Mullin plunged into the abyss and said: '*Ar ais ar stailc ocrais*' ('Back on hunger strike.') I was aghast at the suggestion, as were Bik and Jake. Pat, however, was deadly serious. He was a dour, solemn Tyrone man who never baulked at speaking his mind, and his mind was telling him that there was no other way. He had been pressing Bobby and The Dark to let him become one of the first hunger strikers. The fact that he had an ulcer ruled him out of ever being allowed to go on hunger strike, however – but he was a tenacious character who would gladly have seen the thing through.

Ominously, Bobby said nothing. While we argued that this time a hunger strike would certainly mean deaths and there would still be no guarantee of success, Bobby hadn't voiced his opinion. But after a short while, he stopped us and said: '*Sin é, ar ais ar stailc ocrais.*' ('That's it, back on hunger strike.') The wing seemed to become deathly quiet as we wrestled with the gravity of Bobby's words. I felt disbelief and panic.

After he had recovered from his initial shock, Bik intervened and made his opposition to a new hunger strike strikingly clear. Deaths would not necessarily save the situation, he said, and deaths were exactly what lay ahead of us. I outlined the reasons I believed we shouldn't go back down the tortuous road of the hunger strike. Like Bik, I felt that the British would hold firm and that, if anything, the way the first strike had ended, without anything being achieved, would bolster the British and make them more determined not to concede anything. Therefore, in my opinion, the tactic of hunger striking was unsound. Jake Jackson, who was noted for his sharp analytical mind, was of the same opinion as Bik and me.

But Bobby was a headstrong individual who didn't hesitate to take hard decisions, no matter what the personal repercussions. He said that Pat was right and that he could see no other way out of this imbroglio.

The discussion was effectively over. In the IRA, even in jail, the OC's word is law. No matter what the level of opposition, Bobby had the power to overrule everybody. Bobby's parting words were: 'I'm not goin' to like the first thought that comes into my head tomorrow mornin'.'

He left no room for doubting that he would lead the proposed second hunger strike. Bobby had elected himself our Cúchulainn.

Even though Bobby Sands had decided to resume the hunger strike if he got clearance from the Army Council,

he inwardly hoped that, somehow, the British government would move to defuse the situation by, for instance,
conceding on the clothes issue. In mid-January 1981, he
began a series of meetings with the prison governor,
Stanley Hilditch, to see if there was a way out of the
impasse.

They thrashed out a loose agreement. A step-by-step
process began which we hoped would lead to the protest
becoming unnecessary. Hilditch promised that he would
respond with flexibility. The first step entailed two wings
ending the fouling of their cells. Our wing and a wing
from H5 stopped dirtying our cells and were subsequently moved into a clean wing with furniture. Eight
men from each wing were selected to wash themselves,
and families were told to send in civilian clothes for them
to wear, but these were put in storage, to be given to their
owners only when we ended the protest and accepted the
regime, as it existed, unchanged. But we were not going
to change. We were the same political prisoners, and we
were still defiant. The prison authorities never really
understood us.

Although Hilditch spoke of 'flexibility', the reality was
far removed. The bottom line was that the proposals
didn't progress.

There was no alternative but to return to the dirty
protest. On the night of 27 January 1981, at eight o'clock,
we wrecked our cells and destroyed our furniture.

We were moved to a dirty wing and then left all night
in the freezing cold with only a small linen towel each to
keep us warm. The cells were dark and empty, and there
were no mattresses, blankets or water. With the windows
out and the heat turned off, we shivered in the arctic
conditions.

As ever, Bobby tried to keep up morale, but nobody

wanted a sing-song or was in the mood for banter. It was the worst night of my life up till then. The minutes passed like hours as Scull and I beat our arms against our backs to keep warm. The coldness of the floor made our feet sore while we stood at each side of the window and prayed for the dawn. We took turns sitting on the upturned pisspot and lifting our feet into the air to keep them off the cold floor. A pisspot is not the most comfortable of seats, though, and our legs got tired, so we were forced to stand again. Was the dawn ever going to come? The clock seemed to be marching backwards.

At ten o'clock the next morning, after fourteen hours without heat or water, we were like frozen mammoths, barely able to talk because of our chattering teeth. We still had no bedding, but every man jack of us had put in a request to see the doctor and the governor. When asked why we wanted to see the governor, we explained that we wanted to get 'board forms' (request forms) so that we could see our solicitors about the inhumanity of the regime. Five minutes later, we got the bedding. Never were an emaciated mattress, a couple of filthy blankets and a drink of water more appreciated. I quickly got under the blankets, and fell asleep within seconds.

Bob wrote a comm that day to Liam Óg telling him: 'The boys are exhausted, the wing's like a morgue – all asleep.' He went on to say that, if we hadn't all put a request to the governor for board forms to see our solicitors, 'We'd have been sitting fuckin' foundered till tonight. Man near collapsed here with cold and exhaustion.'

At eleven o'clock, we were awoken to see the governor. Bleary-eyed and dead on my feet, I told Scull that the governor could 'go an' get stuffed', but duty, as ever, prevailed.

Bobby told Liam Óg that, at midday, 'To rub it in, they put our dinner out, left it sitting for half an hour, then gave it to us freezing cold.'

The screws had laughed that morning at the frozen wretches grabbing the blankets, but those boys could not comprehend what made us tick. They never realised that the more they laughed and the more pain they heaped on us, the more we drew on each other. The brutality only ensured that the famous blanket *esprit de corps* made us soulmates rather than mere cellmates: we became indestructible.

Bobby got down to business and set about choosing those who would join him on hunger strike. As the names of volunteers came in from the other blocks, he scanned them for individuals whom he wanted to follow him. The names he was seeking were on the list of volunteers. They were Frank Hughes, from south Derry, and Raymond McCreesh, from south Armagh. The INLA also wanted to be represented on the hunger strike; their OC, Patsy O'Hara from Derry, was going to lead them.

Comms were being exchanged at fever pitch between the Army Council and the prison leadership. The Council once again set its face against a new hunger strike on the grounds that it might imperil the whole war effort. While not withholding permission for a hunger strike – which they could well have done – they made it absolutely clear that they believed that deaths were certain, and if any hesitation to die on the part of the hunger strikers resulted in last-minute vacillation, the campaign in general would be dealt a potentially mortal blow. The options were clear: if we still wanted to go on hunger strike, we had to realise that it was die or kill the struggle. But this time both the Army Council and the prisoners knew that there could be no cover-up as there had been at the end of the first hunger strike. Our support base would see through another round of deception (although that deception was necessary to give us the breathing space to try and chart another way out of our predicament – witness Bobby's efforts to get Governor Hilditch to move to defuse the situation). This time we would either emerge with the nucleus of political status or we would not; if we didn't, it would be transparent to all that our efforts had failed.

The Army Council had the power to say no to a hunger strike, and such an order would have been accepted. For IRA men, an order from the Army Council is absolute. The seven members of the Council have a duty to consider the broader picture: the struggle in general was of primary importance to them – and rightly so. But the Army Council was also in a hard place. The last thing its members wanted to do was to abandon their comrades to the prison regime and see them depicted as criminals. They too felt that they were under a great moral strain.

Bobby remained resolute, forcefully pointing out that there was no other route for us to take. Since he was going to lead the strike himself, he would make certain that, if deaths were to occur, he could be relied on to go all the way. I believe that he had no illusions about what lay ahead for him. His would be a lonely, one-way journey; unlike Lot's wife, he would not look back.

In the end, a sympathetic leadership acceded to Bobby's request with heavy hearts. The fast was set to begin on 1 March 1981, the fifth anniversary of the introduction of the criminalisation policy; the count-down began.

The Army Council informed us that operations would not be scaled down and that the war would go on. They said this because they wanted to isolate the prisons issue from the overall struggle. While Bobby may have convinced the Army Council that he would die if necessary, and that this would have removed the immediate threat to the continuance of the armed struggle, the Council still had a duty to take a longer-term view of the conflict. The non-scaling-down of operations was akin to a comprehensive insurance policy: it was essentially a get-out clause.

In February, Bobby had approached me to take on the job of public-relations officer from Bik, who was to be the new Block OC. I had an obligation to do all in my power to help the situation and felt duty-bound to accept the job. Then Bik told me about the Army Council's reluctance to allow the hunger strike to go ahead and the intricacies of the Council's deliberations.

Bobby was now a much quieter person. The bubbly, energetic individual we had all come to know and love was gone. In his place was a solemn, sober person who was more reflective and inward-looking. The similarities between Bobby and The Dark were striking: the grin was sometimes there, but the eyes were jaded, as if they were looking into a distant world. Bobby's manner was gentle, even docile, but there was no disguising the steel-like determination underneath. This was a man coming to terms with his own mortality. Something told me that he would see this journey through to the bitter end.

13

The lesson of collective decision-making, which had been a feature of the first hunger strike, had certainly been absorbed. As a result, the format for the second strike would bear no similarity to that of the first. Rather than several men going on the strike simultaneously and reaching a critical point together, one person at a time would embark on it. The logic of this was that one man on his own, uninfluenced by anyone else, would be more inclined to die. To have other people's lives in your hands was an intolerable predicament for anyone to be in – as we had found out with The Dark. This way there was no ambiguity. The decision to live or die would be the individual's.

I don't know where the one-man-at-a-time tactic originated (although I suspect it was Bobby who came up with it), but in terms of ensuring that the hunger strikers would stick rigidly to their fast, it was ingenious. Like the tactics for the first hunger strike, however, it contained within it a deadly cancer – only this time the cancer had mutated to take on a different, more extreme, form. The one-man-at-a-time approach was specifically designed to put maximum pressure on the man coming behind a dead hunger striker, placing a moral prerogative on his shoulders to follow his comrade to the grave. Yet while this innovation was tactically brilliant in terms of ensuring the continuity of the hunger strike, it could not fail also to bring about an intellectual vacuum that would inexorably lead to a blind, dogged determination on the part of the hunger strikers not to let down those who had already died. This tumour would manifest itself in the later stages of the hunger strike when some hunger strikers came to the realisation that there was no chance of gaining the five demands, yet went to their deaths undaunted.

To offset the possibility of hunger strikers making conclusive decisions on any package that may come from the British, the strikers were told that they were not permitted to negotiate with anyone from the Northern Ireland Office or to pass judgment on any proposals without our OC, Bik McFarlane, being present. Should the possibility of such talks arise, Bik would then insist that Gerry Adams and Danny Morrison be present. (This ensured that the dispute would have to be sanctioned by the wider republican movement.) This mechanism was designed to counter the breakdown in the command structure which had occurred at the end of the first hunger strike.

My immediate task was to draw up the statement announcing the start of the hunger strike, to be released when Bobby started his fast on 1 March 1981. This wasn't difficult because I had been writing more or less the same stuff as part of our propaganda campaign for the past two years. Still, I needed to be focused. The statement had to stir nationalists and persuade them to support our cause. The justice of our case was self-evident, but the people were exhausted from the first hunger strike, and I had the unenviable responsibility of rallying them once again.

BLANKETMEN

We, the Republican POWs in the H-Blocks of Long Kesh, and our comrades in Armagh Prison, are entitled to and hereby demand political status, and we reject today, as we have consistently rejected every day since September 14th 1976, when the Blanket protest began, the British government's attempted criminalisation of ourselves and our struggle.

Five years ago this day, the British government declared that anyone arrested and convicted after March 1st 1976, was to be treated as a criminal and no longer as a political prisoner. Five years later, we are still able to declare that the criminalisation policy, which we have resisted and suffered, has failed.

If a British government experienced such a long and persistent resistance to a domestic policy in England, then that policy would almost certainly be changed. But not so in Ireland, where its traditional racist attitude blinds its judgement to reason and persuasion.

Only the loud voice of the Irish people and world opinion can bring them to their senses, and only a hunger strike, where lives are laid down as proof of our political convictions, can rally such opinion and present the British with the problem that, far from criminalising the cause of Ireland, their intransigence is actually bringing attention to that cause.

We have asserted that we are political prisoners and everything about our country, our arrests, interrogations, trials and prison conditions show that we are politically motivated and not motivated by selfish reasons or for selfish ends. As a further demonstration of our selflessness and the justness of our cause, a number of our comrades, beginning today with Bobby Sands, will hunger strike to the death unless the British government abandons its criminalisation policy and meets our demand for political status.

This text was the product of efforts by Danny Morrison, the republican press officer, and myself. I was happy to have Danny's experience to call on in composing such an important statement. Still, there was a lump in my throat when I got to the phrase 'will hunger strike to the death'. The meaning of those words crushed my soul, for I knew that this time people would die, and my friend Bobby was going to be the first.

Amongst his many talents, Bobby was a gifted songwriter. Bik and he had composed a brilliant ballad about a poteen-maker called McIlhatton from the Glens of Antrim, but I had been pressing Bobby for some time to write out the words of another song he had composed, entitled 'Sad Song for Susan'. On the first morning of the hunger strike, he finally obliged.

At the bottom, he wrote: 'There y'are, Risteard, fresh from the heart. For what it's worth, I wrote this one rainy afternoon on remand in H1 when I had the fine company of a guitar to pluck out this tune, so *sin é* [that's it]. Is Joany crying?'

Joany was the name of Scull's girlfriend. Bobby knew that Scull would have a heavy heart, as we all had, at his going on hunger strike. Bobby and Scull had shared a cell for months and were close friends.

I studied Bobby's poignant words for ages, wondering who Susan was. Bobby was separated, but his wife's name wasn't Susan, and when I asked him at Mass that Sunday, he just smiled and looked ahead as if delving into a lost world of distant – and happier – memories. Unlike the other material things in his life, it was something he could not share with us. Susan was a lucky girl to have known Bobby.

On the day after Bobby started the hunger strike, the dirty protest stopped. It had run its course and had succeeded in highlighting our demands. Nothing was to divert attention from the bigger picture.

That first hot shower was divine: no words can describe my feelings as I washed off three and a half years of dirt – but nothing could wash away the spirit of protest. We were what we always had been – political prisoners – only now our adversaries could see the whites of our eyes as we stared into theirs, our defiance pitted against their shame.

Because of the tats in our hair, it was impossible to run a comb through it, so everybody had to get a skinhead haircut. With the haircuts and the hairless chins, we found each other's appearance hilarious. The common phrase was: 'God, you're an ugly child.' Most of us couldn't remember our original selves, and we had lost a lot of weight since the beginning of the blanket protest. It was like being introduced to a new set of people.

There was a definite lack of enthusiasm for the hunger strike outside the jail. The marches and demonstrations were not drawing the numbers needed to seriously worry the Brits, and this was a major concern for us. Our only hope of influencing the Thatcher government was to mobilise national and international opinion, but that didn't seem to be happening.

On Bobby's birthday, 9 March, we gave him a concert through our cell doors, and for a while he was his old self, ribbing and making jokes. This was Bobby at his brilliant best: his body was facing emaciation, but his mind was full of liberation. We loved him, but more importantly, he loved us. At the end he thanked us and gave a speech from his cell door, during which he expressed his pride at having known us and reaffirmed his commitment to the hunger strike and his belief that he wasn't going to 'let anyone down'.

I had known Father Denis Faul from the days of internment, when he would visit the Cages to say Mass. He was a fierce critic of the establishment and had co-written several books with Father Raymond Murray condemning British torture and human-rights abuses in the North. He also wasn't slow to criticise the IRA when atrocities were committed in its name, but that was Denis – a human-rights campaigner who cherished his independence.

He had been in to see Bobby and had tried to convince him that more time was needed to move the British. Bobby was firm: he believed that the Thatcher government had had ample opportunity to settle the matter reasonably, and to delay any further was a waste of time. The British, he was convinced, wanted the confrontation.

Before Father Faul left, Bobby quoted Jesus Christ: 'Greater love hath no man than to lay down his life for his friends.' A sorrowful Father Faul concluded that Bobby was acting in good conscience and that there was no answer to the quoted words. It must have been a touching experience for both men.

At Mass on the three Sundays that Bobby remained in

our wing, he, Bik, Jake Jackson, Pat Mullin and I huddled behind the hot plate (an oven used to keep the food warm) discussing the situation. Bobby's main concern was to ensure that we would not accept a half-baked settlement just because he was at death's door. He made it crystal clear that he was to be allowed to die if that happened. Just what that half-baked solution might be wasn't discussed, but it was taken as read that he was referring to a situation where the clothes demand alone was being offered, along with some minor adjustments to the prison regime. At the time, I was more concerned with enjoying my last moments with Bobby than with focusing on what constituted a half-baked settlement. Sure, there were technical things that needed our immediate attention – lines of communication being one of them – but we never got down to the fine detail of what the complexion of a settlement with honour could possibly be, or what our minimum requirements were. We had made five demands that, on the face of it, needed no explanation.

Bobby had other concerns, which he relayed to the outside leadership in a comm to Liam Óg on 16 March. He asked them to consider the possibility that, should the three proposed IRA hunger strikers die first (himself, Frank Hughes and Raymond McCreesh), then only Patsy O'Hara would be left. Patsy was a member of a separate, autonomous organisation, the Irish National Liberation Army, and Bobby was worried that, if that happened, the IRA would lose control of the situation. He wanted the Army Council to consider putting a fourth IRA hunger striker on the fast behind Patsy.

> Comrade, now here's a point that's worrying me: in the event of me, Frankie or Raymond dying, you'll

have no one left to work with and you know who'd be left behind [Patsy O'Hara]. Just thought that someone left behind him would be a safeguard. Let's face it, comrade, it may well happen like that.

Frank Hughes joined Bobby on hunger strike after a fortnight, two days before Bobby wrote his comm to Liam Óg. Hughes was a legend in IRA circles. He had trekked the fields of south Derry for years fighting the British in almost open combat and was caught only after a firefight with 14 Intelligence Company, an elite section of the British army which was renowned for set-piece killings (where IRA Volunteers walked into a carefully constructed trap and were wiped out). During the firefight, he had killed one of their men before being seriously wounded himself. Such was the strength of the man that he underwent surgery to shorten his leg without anaesthetic in case he might give away any information under sedation.

Patsy O'Hara from Derry and Raymond McCreesh from south Armagh joined the hunger strike on the same day, 22 March. I didn't know either of those two lads personally, but I read their comms confirming that they were prepared to go on hunger strike. There was a chilling determination about the comms, as both men committed themselves to hunger strike unto death if necessary.

On Sunday 23 March, just before Mass, Bobby told us that he was being moved to the prison hospital. He shook hands with me and smiled. It was the sad smile of leave-taking, the smile of an emigrant destined never to return. I knew in my heart that I would never see Bobby again, and I think he saw that in my eyes. I tried to think of something to say that would give him even a little chink of hope, but thought better of it. 'Ya can't kid the kid,' as he used to say. With heavy hearts, we parted.

Before he left the wing, he called to our cell door and spoke to us through the side of it, bidding Scull and me farewell. Then he was gone.

14

An event had occurred some weeks earlier that was to transform our fortunes. Frank Maguire, the independent Westminster MP for Fermanagh/South Tyrone, had died unexpectedly on 5 March. Frank was a republican of the old school; during the fifties IRA campaign, he had commanded an IRA unit and been interned in Crumlin Road Jail. He had successfully held the Fermanagh/South Tyrone seat from 1974 and was effectively a republican abstentionist politician, although he sometimes voted for the Labour government when its majority in the House of Commons was under threat. Maguire had unreservedly supported our five demands and had championed our cause at every opportunity.

There is some dispute about who came up with the idea of putting Bobby Sands's name forward as a by-election candidate for the vacant seat. Republicans believe that it was Jim Gibney, a leading Sinn Féin activist, a member of the National H-Blocks Committee and a man who was central to the formation of republican policy during the hunger strike. Others are convinced that the suggestion was the brainchild of Bernadette Devlin McAlliskey, the former civil-rights MP for Mid-Ulster and also a member of the National H-

Blocks Committee. Whoever's suggestion it was, the republican leadership, after some debate, endorsed the concept, but only on the grounds that, for Bobby's name to go forward, there would have to be a clear nationalist field because the SDLP was likely to field a candidate and there were other potential independent candidates.

The main problem was that Frank's younger brother, Noel, was reckoned to be his political heir, and if Bobby was to have a chance of beating the Ulster Unionist candidate, the former party leader Harry West, the least he needed was for Noel Maguire to refrain from running. While others signalled an interest in the seat, it was Noel who first had to be convinced that he shouldn't put his name forward as a candidate. After much persuasion and 'conscience-baiting', principally from Sinn Féin Vice-President Gerry Adams and Jim Gibney, Noel agreed to support Bobby's candidature.

Austin Currie, a politician from the SDLP, did us no favours. His party leadership had not put up a candidate to oppose Frank Maguire at the previous election, in 1979, in order not to split the nationalist vote. But with Maguire dead, the SDLP initially stated that it would run a candidate come what may. Because of the life-and-death situation in the H-Blocks, however, they felt compelled to withdraw, not least because of huge grass-roots pressure from nationalists. Currie, who would have been the official SDLP candidate, intimated that he would defy party policy and stand anyway, but in the end he withdrew in favour of Bobby. Our leadership had done a magnificent job of clearing the field.

Fermanagh/South Tyrone was the scene of a whirlwind campaign. There were only nine days to polling day when Bobby's nomination papers were lodged, and republicans from all over Ireland rallied to the call for help. Doors that had never seen a politician were soon being rapped.

What we didn't know was where the substantial SDLP vote was going to go. The party leadership told their supporters to boycott the election, which from their point of view was understandable, given the moral blackmail to which the republican movement had subjected them. But we shed no tears over that; there was the matter of whether Bobby Sands would live or die, and morality dictated that the SDLP had to give way to him. This issue was bigger than party politics.

While the election campaign continued outside the jail, the prison leadership concentrated on firming up our hunger-strike strategy. Bik was a prolific writer, but he had taken on an awesome responsibility when he became OC, and he needed a sounding board. Perhaps it was because I was only two cells away from him, or because I was the block's public-relations officer, but I was chosen to be the person on whom Bik would test his ideas.

Our focus naturally had to be on the long term, but our immediate concern was to decide how the hunger strike would develop if the British government allowed the first four hunger strikers to die. We were of the opinion that, at the very least, we had to seek replacements as each hunger striker died, if for no other reason than to maintain the pressure on the British and to convince them that we were prepared to let a fifth hunger striker die, and a sixth – and however many it took to defeat them.

We believed that the British assumed that it was a four-man strike and that after the fourth death it would end, and they would be out of the woods. We needed to convince them that they would not get off so easily and that only an honourable settlement would lift the siege.

In private, however, Bik and I had decided that, if the fourth man died, come what may, we were going to end the protest before the fifth hunger striker died. The replacements were a bluff, and we accepted that if the British still hadn't moved as the fifth hunger striker was facing death, then they were never going to move. We set about selecting replacements, the first being Joe McDonnell, who would take Bobby's place in the event of his death. Other than Jake Jackson and Pat Mullin and the outside leadership, nobody knew anything about our strategy; the ordinary Blanketman wasn't informed.

The selection process entailed a detailed consideration of the other 60–70 volunteers for the hunger strike. We focused on men we knew. Those we had known personally came under the spotlight: men who had a fairly long republican pedigree, had displayed more than their fair share of resistance to the British, had either been interned or been in the Cages and had pleaded with us to let them be on the hunger strike – as many did.

It was all done in a dispassionate way; the only qualifications needed to get on hunger strike were a clean bill of health physically and a media-friendly persona (if such a thing existed for republican prisoners). Some of our men would have been propaganda nightmares because of the charges they were on, such as sectarian killings, and we had to eliminate them from consideration. Others had medical problems, such as ulcers, which could prove life-threatening in the early stages of a hunger strike; their applications were politely but firmly turned down. It may have seemed ruthless, but there was no advantage to be had in people dying needlessly from stomach complaints. If we were to lose our most cherished comrades in an act of political protest, the hunger strike alone had to be the cause of their deaths. We wanted fewer deaths, not more or quicker ones.

Each potential replacement received a comm from the Army Council telling that prisoner to take time to mull over his decision. They were also told that no one would think any less of them if they changed their minds, but they had to understand that to proceed with their decision meant only one thing – their death.

I can remember most of the more exhilarating moments in my life – those unforgettable times when I was ecstatically happy. Being released from jail was such a time; getting married was another; and the birth of my daughter, Bernadette, was a true red-letter day. The 1981 Fermanagh/South Tyrone by-election ranks with them all. Despite all the negative campaigning from the Official Unionist candidate, and with the British sticking in their 'tuppenceworth', Bobby Sands was elected the Member of Parliament for the constituency. Bik, who had been listening on his crystal radio, quietly conveyed the news that 30,092 people had turned out to vote for Bobby, giving him a majority of 1,446 votes over Harry West, the Ulster Unionist candidate. The enormous vote for Bobby demolished the British assertion that the prisoners had no support.

Our leadership and supporters had pulled off a magnificent coup: they had achieved the unthinkable. In a comm to Liam Óg, Bik summed up how much we appreciated their efforts:

Comrade, What a day – a real super effort!! Don't know whether to laugh, shout or cry. The news was greeted here in silent jubilation (we are very security conscious you know!!) . . . Congrats to one and all, you wonderful people. We really showed them. Take care and God bless . . . Up the good old RA and other outrageous outbursts. Nite, nite and God speed. Bik.

Bobby's victory was a tacit acknowledgement that the IRA had the right to fight a political war to rid the country of foreign rule. Harry West, and even Thatcher herself, had said that a vote for Sands was a vote for the IRA. So be it. The people had spoken and returned this IRA man to represent them.

The reason the news was greeted 'in silent jubilation' was because we didn't want to alert the screws to the fact that we had radios in the wings. It was a hard order to obey, though, and it was harder still to keep the smiles off our faces when the screws returned in sullen mood from their afternoon break to do a head-count.

Was this breakthrough the answer to our prayers, I wondered. Were the British capable of ignoring the vote? Were they so entrenched that they couldn't even see the ramifications of it? Would they let a member of their own parliament die on hunger strike? One thing was certain: the British never expected, or allowed for, such a development. Bobby Sands MP – it sounded good to me.

We received the newspapers the next morning (we were still on protest, but the British in their infinite mercy had begun to provide us with the morning papers), and they made fine reading. The *Daily Express*, a Tory paper, summed it up: 'ELECTED: THE HON. MEMBER FOR VIOLENCE.' I loved that. Another told the voters that 'Their attendance at Mass this morning is as corrupt as Judas's kiss.' These were some boys to lecture Irish people about Judas's kiss! Democracy was a magnificent edifice when it suited the British, but how dare people in Ireland insult democracy by electing a candidate not to their liking. How dare they elect someone who had fought against their army on the streets of Belfast. How dare they expect that the same rules would apply to their MP as to others. It was such a pleasure to see them squirm in discomfort. Their arrogance was awesome.

Bobby Sands was now, at the same time, a political prisoner, a Member of Parliament, a hunger striker and a 'criminal' – truly, he was a man for all seasons.

15

Bobby sent a comm to Bik, which I saw, expressing his opinion that the by-election wouldn't change the British at all and that, as sure as day turns into night, he was going to die.

He certainly had his finger on the pulse, for, within days, Margaret Thatcher made it plain that Bobby's election to Westminster changed nothing. While on a visit to Saudi Arabia, she was asked to comment on Bobby's victory and proclaimed that: 'A crime is a crime is a crime.' Even more bizarrely, the British wanted to disbar Bobby from becoming a Member of Parliament. They changed their minds only when they realised that another hunger striker would fight the seat and that they would in all likelihood have to go through the embarrassment all over again.

The Army Council had decided to set up a committee to monitor the progress of the hunger strike. It included Gerry Adams, Danny Morrison, Jim Gibney and Liam Óg. Adams was charged with the task of representing the committee's, and thus the Army Council's, opinion. He told Bik of their collective thinking in a comm in late April: they were very much against a protracted hunger strike. Their fear was that, if the British government hadn't moved before the first four men died, then they would not move at all, and the committee wanted at all costs to avoid a fifth hunger striker dying. David Beresford, author of *Ten Men Dead*, was told by leading republicans when he was researching his book that the committee had ruled out replacing the first four with a separate and second 'squad': it would be too much like starting a second and third hunger strike. Instead, they agreed with the prisoners that if a hunger striker died he would be replaced with another on an individual basis. But if the first four hunger strikers died, they would effectively have another squad of replacements. So would it be worth going beyond the first four? Bik figured not. If public pressure failed to move the government by the time the first four had died, the republican movement would have effectively shot its bolt. And after four, with the authorities still adamant, more deaths would start to look like suicide, which would be damaging for the movement.

While a four-man hunger strike was both the Army Council's and the prison leadership's agreed position, Bik was already looking beyond that and was contemplating the possibility of an alternative destiny. In a comm to Liam Óg on 30 April (five days before Bobby Sands died), he said that, while he agreed with the Army Council's position on a protracted hunger strike, there was more to consider:

> If changing circumstances offer us other avenues which at one time [were] considered infeasible [*sic*] [and] are now considered feasible, we should explore them.

The 'infeasible' was obviously the Army Council's and our shared view of a protracted hunger strike, and the feasible – while not yet practicable or manifest – was Bik playing around with the idea that, somehow, a portent of victory would emerge at some time in the future which would necessitate us having to consider going beyond Joe McDonnell, who would be the fifth hunger striker if Bobby died.

Had such a portent of victory been visible, I would have agreed with Bik and opted for a protracted hunger strike. It has to be understood that the prisoners were in this to win and were of the mentality that, should victory appear on the horizon, then we, as the jail leadership, were duty-bound to go for it – even if this meant more deaths than we had previously allowed for. Having said that, I couldn't imagine what those 'changing circumstances' might be.

After the by-election, the British pretended that they were being flexible: three Irish members of the European Parliament, Síle de Valera, Neil Blaney and Dr John O' Connell, were allowed in to Long Kesh to see Bobby. The Irish delegation's sentiments were good, but they had nothing to offer.

Bobby was reaching a decisive stage in his hunger strike. He had to sleep on a sheepskin rug on a waterbed because his skin was breaking out in sores. His eyesight was fading, and he was very weak.

I tried to imagine what it must be like for him to be aware that, in a little time, he wouldn't be of this earth any more. Surely he would think that his God had forsaken him, and that at only twenty-seven years of age he was about to fulfil his life's purpose. Did Bobby regret the way his life had panned out? Did he regret that

'Susan' and he weren't together any more? What would Susan have thought about his predicament if she were still with him? Would she have blamed us for putting him on this road, or would she have understood that it was the British who were the real culprits?

These questions only reinforced my deep sense of helplessness and misery over Bobby's situation. It was worse than terrible knowing that this man was just waiting to die and that there was nothing any of us could do about it.

Charles Haughey, the Irish Taoiseach, needed an end to the hunger strike so that he could call a general election. The Fermanagh/South Tyrone by-election had demonstrated that there was a groundswell of support for the hunger strike amongst the Irish people, and Haughey was deeply worried that hunger-strike candidates would stand in the general election and win seats. His Fianna Fáil party had only a tiny majority in the Dáil, and he was trying to avoid his government's fall from power.

Haughey came up with the idea of involving the European Commission for Human Rights to bring about an end to the hunger strike. The European Commission's role was to investigate complaints and mediate between the parties. The Commission had been involved in the dispute before and had rejected our claims to be political prisoners in June 1980. At the same time, it expressed concern 'at the inflexible approach of the State authorities, which has been concerned more to punish offenders against prison discipline than to explore ways of resolving such a serious deadlock'. To involve the Commission, Haughey needed the prisoners to lodge a complaint against the British government, and Bobby was the obvious choice to do so. Haughey persuaded Bobby's sister, Marcella, to sign a complaint against the British, and two Commission officials were dispatched from Strasbourg to Long Kesh.

Our reaction was that this was an attempt to circumvent our procedures for negotiation. The prisoners and the Army Council had agreed that Bik, Gerry Adams and Danny Morrison should attend any negotiations about ending the hunger strike. But the European commissioners also had procedures, and they did not include witnesses, so that ruled out the attendance of Bik, Adams and Morrison at any meetings with Bobby. Bobby stood firm on the attendance of our negotiators, and the commissioners went back to Strasbourg. It was the first taste of the procedural minefield that would haunt the hunger strike.

Then the Pope's secretary, Fr John Magee, came to Long Kesh. He had nothing to offer except prayers and a large crucifix for Bobby. While I had every faith in the power of prayer, I had hoped that the Vatican would have had more to offer.

There was now little doubt about it: the British were going to let Bobby die. Bik went to see him and he returned shattered. Bik was a man who felt deeply about life, death and principles and who showed his compassion in his letters to me and in our conversations out of our cell windows. He was like a lighthouse, isolated and vulnerable, battered by the ferocious waves of British imperialism. He was not emotionally immune to the charge, emanating from the British gutter press, that he was a sectarian bigot: they discovered that he had been sentenced to life imprisonment for blowing up a loyalist bar in which it was thought that leading members of the

Ulster Volunteer Force were having a meeting. Unfortunately, the IRA intelligence had got it wrong, and those who died were ordinary Protestants, rather than UVF members. That didn't matter to the moguls of Fleet Street; to them, there was a chink in Bik's armour.

The British media were also accusing Bik of cowardice for not going on hunger strike himself. While there was no way of knowing it, nothing could be further from the truth. The fact was that Bik had been tormenting the The Dark to be allowed to go on the first hunger strike, and he had also been very adamant that he wanted to stand beside Bobby and the boys in the second hunger strike. This man was no coward. Still, I'm sure the nails sank deep into his heart. Despite the media jibes, Bik knew that propaganda alone would decide the outcome of this battle.

I tried to support Bik when he was, naturally, down. Nevertheless, after that last visit with Bobby, when Bobby's last words to him were, 'I'm dyin', Bik,' I felt I could almost touch his anguish. There was nothing I could say that could ease Bik's pain. We all felt the same, but at least, unlike the pitiful position that Bik was in, the rest of us didn't have to see Bobby. I didn't want to see him; I much preferred to remember Bobby as I had known him – as the bubbly character, the heart of the protest and the dynamic brother I had come to know and love. He was our friend.

On 3 May, Marty McManus, who was in the cell between Bik and me, rapped on the cell wall and called me down to the pipes, where we could talk quietly through a small aperture. He then told me that the prison chaplain had just visited Bik in his cell and informed him that his father had died. My heart went out to my big friend. I called him up to the window to tell him how sorry I was, and he dolefully replied: 'Rick, I know.' We left it at that; there was nothing more I could say. Could it possibly get any worse for him? Not only had he to face the prospect that his great pal Bobby would be dead very soon, but on top of that he had to deal with the dreadful news that his father had died. To make matters worse, he hadn't had a clue that his father was ill because he had never taken visits from his family since he had come on the protest, and there had been no hint of his father being in poor health in any of the monthly letters he received from home. (Obviously his mother didn't want to worry him.) I was devastated for my friend.

16

At 1.06 AM on 5 May 1981, after sixty-six days on hunger strike, the spirit of Bobby Sands left his earthly body on its journey to another world.

Bik got the news on his radio. Big Marty McManus tapped the pipes and whispered solemnly that Bobby had just died. It was over for my buddy: no more pain, no more torture.

I was expecting his death, but I was still desolate. Never in my life had I felt such torment; it was as if my own life-force had been expelled from my body. I lay silently on my bed recalling the good times I had enjoyed with Bobby, finding both succour and emptiness in the man's life and death.

Scull was the same. I tried to comfort him, but I could only stare vacantly as he wept. I put my arm around his shoulder. All the while, I was finding it impossible to hold back the tears myself. A light of inspiration had been extinguished, but an eternal flame of valour had been lit, a flame that inspires the Spartacuses of this world to persevere for justice to this day.

Cúchulainn had manned the Bearna Mhaol and fulfilled his promise. Another Cúchulainn, Joe McDonnell, replaced Bobby on hunger strike.

The next day, not a sound could be heard on the wing. Even the screws were silent as they went about their duties. Perhaps they expected us to attack them, but they were wrong. That would have achieved nothing and would have deflected attention from Bobby's death.

Ralphie Gilmore, our Class Officer, told one of the boys who had a visitor that Bobby was a man of great principle. It was as close as a screw dared go in praise of any of us, and it was appreciated.

I had to get a death notice ready for the local paper. I wanted to highlight Bobby's philosophy of life:

> They have nothing in their whole imperial arsenal that can break the spirit of one Irishman who doesn't want to be broken.

Bobby had drawn this quote from Leon Uris's novel *Trinity* and had adopted it as his own.

The wing had never been the same after Bobby's birthday concert, but now his death had drained everybody. In the aftermath of his death not a word was heard out of the doors, and the men delved into thier own encyclopaedia of memories. Even the implementation of the five demands would not have lifted morale.

Outside, there was mayhem on the streets. Not since internment had there been such a violent public reaction to a situation engineered by British government policy-makers, as widespread rioting convulsed the North. Black flags were erected in nationalist areas throughout Ireland.

The next day, the Belfast IRA shot dead Constable Philip Ellis at a peace-line barrier on the Duncairn Road in north Belfast. The day after, a fourteen-year-old Protestant schoolboy, Desmond Guiney, was killed when nationalist rioters on the New Lodge Road in Belfast stoned his father's milk float, sending it out of control and crashing into a lamp-post. This poor boy was only helping his father at work. He knew nothing of politics or civil strife. Eric Guiney, the boy's father, died six days later from his injuries.

The Army Council had told us before Bobby died that it would not overreact to his death. The thinking was that the British, who had drafted in hundreds of extra troops, were hoping to draw the IRA into open conflict. Such a development would have been disastrous and would have played right into their hands. We were a guerrilla army of a few hundred men and women; they could call on tens of thousands of troops to oppose us in such a situation.

After Bobby died, a comm came in from Gerry Adams informing us that the movement was having major problems directing the enormous amount of support and energy that the hunger strikes were generating. Adams's view was that we lacked 'middle leadership' – which, when translated, meant that we were getting enormous support in many areas of the North, but in most of these areas we weren't organised. In fact, in some regions there was no republican structure. Thousands of people were on the streets at times, and republicans needed to harness those people into an organised, anti-imperialist body, under the aegis of the republican movement.

We marked Bobby's death with a simple but dignified parade at our cell doors that night. Bik called everyone to attention, and during a heartbreaking two minutes' silence, we paid our last respects to a giant amongst giants. Behind him, other giants stood, ready to take his place. We had to recover and prepare to support them in their coming battle. While we did not know it then, Frank Hughes was only a week away from joining Bobby.

Bobby's funeral was expected to be a big affair. We waited for Bik to tell us the news from his crystal set. As soon as the screws left for their afternoon tea, he set up the radio. Within seconds, he said: 'Ó'Rathaigh [a slang interpretation of my surname in Irish], guess?' I knew that he wanted me to guess the numbers at the funeral in Belfast.

'Cut it out, Bikso. How many?'

'Would you believe, a hundred thousand?'

I almost collapsed. One hundred thousand of our people were walking down the Falls Road behind Bobby's coffin. Never in my life had I been so proud. Who, I asked myself, could ever defeat us?

Frank Hughes died a week later. The centurion's lance was being plunged deeper into our sides. The Peelers did not allow the coffin carrying Frank's remains to be taken to west Belfast, where thousands of people waited to pay homage to a legendary IRA man. Instead, they forced the undertakers to drive through loyalist areas where stones and bottles were thrown at the hearse. Frank's hearse was not permitted to go through Toombebridge, where a huge crowd of people from south Derry had gathered to pay their last respects to their illustrious leader. Nor was it allowed to enter his native Bellaghy. Frank was much feared by his enemies in life; it appeared that they feared him every bit as much in death. Thirty thousand people attended his funeral. Brendan McLaughlin from north Derry replaced Frank on hunger strike.

On the day that Frank died, the British shot dead

INLA Volunteer Emmanuel McLarnon during a riot in Divis Flats at the bottom of the Falls Road. The INLA claimed that he had died 'on active service'. The next day, fourteen–year-old Julie Livingstone was killed by a British army plastic bullet in Andersonstown. Locals disputed the British army's version of events that a riot was taking place when the plastic bullet hit Julie's head.

Five members of the British security forces died in a six-day period between 13 May and 19 May. (Four were blown up by a landmine outside Camlough in south Armagh.)

Ironically, Raymond McCreesh was a native of Camlough, County Armagh. He had been caught with Paddy Quinn, a former cellmate of mine in H6, while ambushing British in south Armagh. We were informed that once, while Raymond was in a daze, the screws had offered him milk. They alleged that he had drunk it, thus ending his hunger strike. Raymond was unaware of where he was and thought he was in Scotland at the time. It was an unscrupulous attempt to undermine his hunger strike when the man was not fully *compos mentis*. When he became conscious again, he still refused food. He died on 21 May.

Patsy O'Hara died on the same day as Raymond. He had been the oc of the Irish National Liberation Army in the prison and had never wavered in his determination to see the hunger strike through. I didn't know Patsy, but I'd met his brother while we were both interned. The family was steeped in republicanism. Despite the fact that he was in a different organisation from me, and that I didn't know him personally, he was my cherished comrade and a colossus amongst his fellow Blanketmen.

The day after Raymond and Patsy died, there were

two more victims of the lethal plastic bullets. Harry Duffy, a forty-four-year-old widower with seven children, had been rioting in Derry's Bogside and had been fatally struck on the left temple by a plastic bullet. Carol Ann Kelly, an eleven-year-old schoolgirl, died that day after having been hit by a plastic bullet three days earlier. As in the case of young Julie Livingstone, locals said that no rioting had been taking place at the time of the schoolgirl's death; the British army said there had been.

Big Kieran Doherty from Andersonstown, Belfast, my friend from internment, replaced Raymond on hunger strike. Kevin Lynch ('Barabbas'), from our wing, who had had the handfuls of salt poured down his throat by the screws, replaced his INLA comrade, Patsy O'Hara, on hunger strike.

Jimmy 'Teapot' McMullan, one of the first Blanketmen, had leadership qualities, and his opinion was highly regarded. He had noticed that the numbers at Raymond and Patsy's funerals were not as large as at Frank's, and that the numbers at Frank's were not as large as at Bobby's. Jimmy thought that the ordinary people outside would eventually become weary of protesting when they did not see any results for their efforts.

Jimmy called Bik and me up to the door almost immediately after Patsy's death and told us that he believed that the British, having allowed four men to die, would let more die and that the hunger strike should be called off. I understood straight away what he was saying and agreed with him. The British would let more hunger strikers die, so crossing the threshold with the fifth hunger striker could not, under any circumstances, be contemplated.

Bik told Jimmy our strategy: we had no intention of

allowing the British to let more men die, but we had to at least maintain the pretence that we would, in the hope of persuading them to grant our five demands.

Immediately after this, however, Bik sent me a comm along the pipes. (Two heating pipes ran the length of both sides of the wing. There was a small space between the pipes and the cell walls through which we could squeeze a flattened piece of cigarette paper.) The comm asked me to consider the possibility that the British would see this through and outlined three possibilities for them:

1. That we were prepared to see large numbers of hunger strikers die to secure our five demands and, accordingly, they would move to end it before Joe McDonnell died.
2. That the replacement strategy was an obvious bluff. In that case, should they wish to settle, they might do so only after Joe had died.
3. That our intentions would not be allowed to be a factor in their considerations. Subsequently, they would shun all attempts at mediation and face us down, no matter how many hunger strikers died.

It was a harrowing analysis of the situation. While Bik wasn't saying that we had shifted our position on not letting Joe McDonnell die, he was no longer ruling it out of the limited range of options available to us.

Bik's presentation was nothing if not accurate. But what it did was illustrate candidly that we had no magic wand or pearls of divine wisdom with which we could fully understand on the situation. The only way we could find out if the British government's resolve was weakening would be if they came and offered us a deal. But would Joe have to die to reach that point? Were there any grounds to think that they would be more inclined to settle after Joe died rather than before? I didn't think so. I decided to try alternative reasoning and put myself in Margaret Thatcher's shoes; the only conclusion I arrived at was that, sooner or later, our protagonists' strength was bound to sap, and they would inevitably cave in to the constant pressure of endless deaths, coupled with dwindling public support, and not a hint of a solution in sight.

So I travelled back to the point where I had started three years earlier, when Blute and I had discussed the possibility of a hunger strike shortly after we had gone on the blanket. I had felt even then that there was little chance of it succeeding.

The crucial question was that, if the British were to remain steadfast, would we be able to recognise that they were not for bending? In other words, at what point would we say enough is enough? Somewhere along this line of reasoning, there was the possibility that what little strategy we had would disintegrate. Would we be able to recognise this if it happened?

I had no immediate answers for Bik and told him so. In fact, I was more confused than ever about the hunger-strike tactic. I was way out of my depth. Trying to anticipate and forestall the British was like counting the grains of sand on a beach – there were incalculable possibilities but no definitive answers, except the obvious one.

What made this conversation with Teapot all the more bizarre was that, a couple of days earlier, while Patsy O'Hara was still in a coma, word came to Bik that

Brendan McLaughlin, who had replaced Frank Hughes, was finding it difficult to keep water down and was in danger of dying prematurely. What we didn't know was that Brendan had a perforated ulcer, and this was the cause of his deterioration. Bik immediately sent a comm to Liam Óg and told him that, if Brendan died in the coming days, we would have to have him replaced.

At face value, it seems that Bik's thinking contradicted our strategy, but the reality was that we reckoned that the pivotal moment in the hunger strike would come when Joe McDonnell was facing death; we thought that then, and only then, would the fog clear and the core issues crystallise. To end the protest before Joe reached that critical point would have thwarted our tactics.

Brendan McLaughlin was ordered to end his hunger strike on 27 May and was replaced by Martin Hurson (Hurson-Boy) from Cappagh, County Tyrone.

Soon after that, Bik raised with me the idea of putting more men on strike. He reckoned that by increasing the number of men on hunger strike we would send a clear message to the British that the only thing on our minds was victory, and that while we regretted the loss of our comrades' lives, we would not let those deaths influence our determination to win political status. After careful consideration, I concluded that we had little to lose. The way I looked at it, we were not going to permit the British to let Joe McDonnell die anyway (although by that stage I was doubting if things would work out as neatly as that), and it could fool them into thinking that there would be no soft landings in this battle.

In a comm to the leadership, Bik asked: 'Can I get the "Big Boy"'s [Gerry Adams's] attitude to escalation as soon as possible and clarification of Tom McElwee as first man?' He went on to ask: 'How many men do we envisage using for this escalation?'

The Army Council approved Tom McElwee as the first man to start the escalation, followed by Paddy Quinn, Raymond McCreesh's friend and co-accused.

By this stage, I was getting severe tension headaches. No amount of tablets seemed to alleviate them as I sat quietly on my bed thinking for hours about the situation. Sleep offered no relief: the opaque, omnipresent images of my dead comrades never left my consciousness. Scull said that while I was asleep I would gnash my teeth and that this was probably why I was getting the headaches. If so, I had good reason to gnash my teeth. I was appalled and bewildered at the position I was in. I was playing a leading role in deciding which of my friends and comrades should risk their lives on a hunger strike in which I didn't believe. Moreover, I was experiencing considerable guilt that I hadn't put my own name forward to go on it. I felt that there was something very callous about administering the day-to-day running of the strike while my own life was never put on the line. On occasion, I was tempted to send a comm up to Bik telling him that I wanted to be the next man to refuse food, but Bernie and wee Bernadette kept pushing themselves into my considerations – and yet Joe McDonnell had kids also and loved his family every bit as much as I loved mine. I remember almost crying with frustration and feeling that I was letting external influences impact on what I believed was the right thing to do. I hated Long Kesh, I hated the hunger strike, and most of all I hated myself.

On the propaganda front, I kept the pressure on the SDLP, the Irish government and the Catholic Church by releasing statements calling for them to come out publicly and support our five demands. For their own reasons, they steadfastly refused to do this, even though they knew that practically the entire nationalist population in Ireland was opposed to the British handling of the situation. They said that to support the five demands would diminish their ability to influence the British. This argument didn't stand up to scrutiny, though: with four men dead, it was obvious that this nationalist bloc had no influence with the British anyway, and the only way they could help us would be to throw their weight wholeheartedly behind us by supporting our demands.

As well as asking the SDLP to publicly support our five demands, we urged them to withdraw from the district council chambers in the North – which the party did not do. Had they done so, the SDLP would have been adopting the republican policy of abstentionism, refusing to take seats in the North's political chambers. From a republican standpoint, constitutional politics meant constitutional compromise; while the SDLP stayed in the chambers, they helped to prop up the British regime in the North and were nothing other than 'little unionists'.

In Dublin, meanwhile, Charles Haughey could postpone the general election no longer and set a date of 11 June 1981 for it to take place. It was another opportunity to highlight our case and was seized on immediately.

Gerry Adams, who was in constant contact with us, was worried that Southerners were insulated from what was going on in the North and that it would be an uphill struggle for us to mobilise popular support there. But he believed that the stakes were too high for us to waver, and we had to throw our cap into the ring by fielding candidates.

A subdued calm had settled over the wing. It was 10 June, and Bik, Jake, Pat and I were preoccupied with the Irish general election and the intensification of the hunger strike. Bik, as usual, was listening to the four o'clock news.

'Ricky, do you remember those bubbles that ya used to talk to me about?' he asked me. 'The Fat Campbell bubbles?'

'Yeah?'

'Well, they've just blown away.'

He told me that Fat and five boys from the 'Murph, along with Joe Doherty from the New Lodge Road in Belfast and Pete Ryan from Tyrone, had shot their way out of Crumlin Road Jail. If ever people deserved a piece of good news, it was the Blanketmen.

The general election in the South was a huge success for the hunger strikers. Kieran Doherty was elected a TD for Cavan/Monaghan, and Paddy Agnew, a Southern Blanketman, was elected for Louth. Other H-Block candidates polled remarkably well too. We were winning the propaganda war, and we revelled in upsetting the establishment.

The first four deaths, preceded by Bobby's election to Westminster, combined with our fantastic election results in the South, led me to conclude that the British criminalisation policy was a dead duck. Outside of the British government, no one believed the 'criminal' fairy tale any longer; the battle against the policy had been effectively won. All that was left was to secure the prison conditions that would manifestly cement our victory.

17

By early June, word had filtered through to us that the
Catholic Church and the SDLP, under the auspices of
the Irish Commission for Justice and Peace, were making
moves to try to end the hunger strike. The five-man
commission consisted of Dermot O'Mahony, the
auxiliary bishop of Dublin; Father Oliver Crilly; Brian
Gallagher, a Dublin solicitor; Jerome Connolly, the
secretary of the commission; and Hugh Logue of the
SDLP.

On 3 June, the commission issued a statement
proposing that, since the women in Armagh Jail had their
own clothes, reason dictated that we should have ours as
well. It was an unanswerable argument, but it had been
made before and the British authorities had ignored it.
The commission stated its belief that there was room for
compromise on the issues of prison work and freedom of
association.

Surprisingly, elements of the British establishment
seemed to agree with the commission, and we began to
think that perhaps something was finally stirring. A
dialogue began on 23 June between the British
government, represented by the minister responsible for

prisons, Michael Allison, and the commission to find common ground.

I personally didn't care about the commission's political make-up. We knew that the Catholic Church and the SDLP were involved, but my attitude was: 'So what?' For the first time since the start of the hunger strike, the British were not dismissing the possibility of a deal being offered, and for me that was a major development. Whatever the political connotations of a settlement, this was secondary to ending the hunger strike successfully.

But Bik was embedded in the republican ethos, and his suspicions were heightened at seeing this intervention by the nationalist constitutional bloc. He thought that the commission's involvement was merely an exercise designed to undermine us, a face-saving endeavour that was inherently working to an anti-republican agenda, whose primary motivation was to gain the ground that had been lost to the republican movement. There was a grain of truth in that analysis, but it is hard to believe that the commission's members were motivated solely by politics: they were also genuinely concerned to see the hunger strike settled on humanitarian grounds.

But no matter where we searched, we could see nothing definite on offer except that we would get to wear our own clothes – and even then the British government had given no indication that they had endorsed this concession. The commission was adamant that the British had moved on the major demands of free association and work; but again, there was no signal from the British that they agreed with the commission's assessment.

Our antagonism towards the commission increased when we became aware that it was putting pressure on the families of the hunger strikers to accept their proposals. It was a *quid pro quo* situation: get your loved ones to end their fast by accepting our concessions; otherwise they will die.

Yet I was still reluctant to see the commission shut out. As the cliché goes, it was the only show in town.

On Sunday 14 June, Father Denis Faul came in to our block to say Mass, and he, Bik, Jake Jackson and I had a discussion on the situation. Father Faul thought we should respond positively to the commission's efforts. We disagreed. We told him our position: there was no solution on the issue of civilian clothes alone – especially now that four men had died. Father Faul said that more than clothes was on offer. We disagreed; we couldn't see anything else. His reply was to insist that there was more, but that we were being too rigid in our demand that Gerry Adams and Danny Morrison should be party to any negotiations. Bik and Father Faul debated the issue. Bik made the point that, if the British government wanted a settlement, they would 'resurrect' James Connolly, the 1916 leader, and bring him into the talks if that suited their needs. Father Faul replied that he thought that sticking to the line that Adams and Morrison should be at any talks was a bigger demand than the other five put together! He said that the British would never accede to it.

In the end we agreed to disagree, but I thought that Bik had gone overboard, and I told him so afterwards. He had displayed his characteristic 'up and at them' side and a 'stuff the Brits' attitude that alienated those outside our circle of comrades. He later told Adams: 'Ricky reckons I went too far.'

Bik's problem was that he viewed the commission as a bunch of charlatans who were interested only in the political gains that could be garnered from ending the hunger strike. This, compounded by his commitment to the republican movement, made for an explosive mixture of passion and hostility towards the commission.

In such a situation, it was imperative to remain detached. Yet how could Bik possibly be anything other than attached? He cared too much; he was too emotionally involved. He had registered his name for the first hunger strike and had been turned down because of the charge for which he had been in prison. Yet he only ever wanted to do what was right by the IRA and his conscience. He wanted to die on hunger strike himself, if need be, and I am certain that he would have died for the five demands.

It was only at a later date, after the ending of the hunger strike, that I realised the import of what Father Faul had said. The demand that Gerry and Danny be present at any negotiations was naïve and politically obstructive. This 'sixth demand', as Father Faul called it during our conversation, increased the stakes enormously and would always have thwarted even a potentially benign British response to our demands. We were, in effect, saying to the British that they had to publicly recognise the moral authority of the republican movement, and thus the IRA, before we would even consider speaking to them about a settlement. Given that their sole purpose in denying us political status in the first place was to propagate the 'criminality' of the war, and that they were referring to Adams and Morrison as 'godfathers', how could they possibly accede to them being involved in negotiations? We were, in effect, making the British an offer they had to refuse.

And if it was impossible for the British to concede any ground on this demand, then it was just as impossible for

us prisoners to get into direct negotiations with them –
even if they wanted to settle – for we were tied body and
soul to this line of negotiation. This precondition had
been imposed before I joined the prison leadership. I
have since sourced it to an Army Council decision made
before the first hunger strike. In attempting to arrive at
some accurate conclusions about this sorry episode in
Irish history, it would be negligent of me not to ask some
questions about the reasoning behind it. Are we to
believe that the IRA leadership did not see the impli-
cations of the decision? Had the Army Council such little
faith in the prison leaders that they could not trust them
to recognise a settlement when they saw one? If the
British allowed Adams and Morrison into the prison to
consider proposals, it would have been impossible to
disguise their deciding influence on whether to accept or
reject those proposals. Had a rejection emerged, the
republican movement would have been seen as the
inflexible party and accordingly been pilloried the length
and breadth of Ireland for letting hunger strikers die. I
doubt if the movement could have recovered from the
criticism; and so, potentially, we would have been
witnessing the funeral dirge of the entire struggle. In
many ways, the republican leadership was lucky that the
British were so dogmatic.

And all the while, Joe McDonnell was edging closer to
death.

In a comm to Adams on 28 June, Bik outlined his
thinking:

Now on the situation and possible Brit move on
Commission's 3 proposals as major undermining
exercise. First of all it is my belief that the alien

elements (Church, SDLP and Haughey) have already succeeded in undermining our position greatly. Families of the hunger strikers appear ready to grab what comes as a feasible settlement. It will, I believe, be attractive to satisfy Church etc of Brit flexibility and in time they will look to us for a response i.e. terminate the hunger strike . . . .If we choose to continue with the hunger strike we will be faced with a situation whereby Joe will die, followed by others and after X amount of deaths public opinion will hammer us into the ground, forcing us to end the hunger strike with nothing to show but deaths that could have been avoided and a shattering defeat into the bargain . . . .If we can combat the undermining successfully and eliminate the prospect of a crushing defeat after further deaths then I feel we should at least maintain our position. I know this could well mean Joe's death and possibly others before we reach a settlement, but if a settlement is obtainable we should try for it. It has been a horrific price to date and may be worse before the finish. Now if we cannot negotiate this hurdle successfully and all the dangers start looming overhead then we must, I believe, give consideration to terminating the hunger strike and salvaging something from Brit concessions.

The tone of Bik's comm clearly indicates that he is looking for direction from the Army Council and effectively handing over control to them in relation to ending or continuing the hunger strike. If the Army Council had replied that we could not negotiate this hurdle successfully, Bik would have ended the hunger strike and attempted to take whatever concessions were on offer. Alternatively, if the Council had told him that a settlement was not attainable, and that the commission's proposals did not represent a settlement and should not be accepted, he still would have ended the hunger strike. The Army Council gave him no advice about either option.

The next day, 29 June, the Northern Ireland Secretary of State, Humphrey Atkins, issued a statement repeating the position that there would be no political status and no changes to the prison regime. He also indicated, however, that the British government wanted a liberal prison regime in the North.

   This statement was completely at odds with the commission's proposals. It rocked us to the core; so much so that Bik wrote to Gerry Adams saying:

> No changes! Are they serious? What sort of people are we dealing with? . . . It appears that they are not interested in simply undermining us, but completely annihilating us.

If Atkins's policy statement was designed to damage our morale, it certainly succeeded. Bik's words accurately reflected our thinking; our cause appeared to be lost. There would be no miraculous parting of the waters. Despite our previous discussions, when we had tried to second-guess the Brits, there was now an emerging consensus: even if we were bluffing, they weren't. In the same comm, Bik asked Adams:

> Can we hope to move these people at all? They are insane – at least Maggie [Thatcher] is. I'm beginning to believe that, *cara* – and it's greatly

worrying me. What way will the families react now?
Just looking at the days ahead – Joe is a cert to die.

Bik was clearly bewildered and alarmed by the inflex-
ibility of the British, but he was definitely not ruling out
the possibility of a protracted hunger strike. He put this
to the Army Council:

> If we can honestly see our objective being achieved,
> then we should maintain our position. I realise that
> as long as our resolve holds then the Brits are always
> going to be the losers. However if they are prepared
> to continue to be losers without conceding our
> demands, then we can only go so far.

On the one hand, Bik believed that the British were
out to 'annihilate' us and that their leader was 'insane'.
On the other, he saw no remedy except continuing with
the hunger strike – but, crucially, only 'If we can honestly
see our objective being achieved'. He clearly harboured
doubts as to whether we could move the British. His
doubts became more transparent when he acknowledged
that the hunger strike could only go 'so far'. The question
that faced us all – prisoners and Army Council alike –
was: when is 'so far' too far? If the British gave no
indication that they were prepared to settle, how many
men would have to die before that question could be
answered?

Like Bik, I was also baffled by Atkins's statement. I
would also have plumped for a protracted hunger strike
had the Army Council stated that the British would in all
probability eventually cave in. But the Council vacillated
and gave no direction either way. Had its members said
that they honestly could not see the prisoners' objectives

being achieved, we would have ended the hunger strike. While the Army Council had no crystal ball, their silence in relation to the future of the hunger strike was telling: it wasn't lost on us that perhaps they thought that we would eventually win through. Otherwise, we reasoned, they would surely tell us to down tools.

After reading the Atkins statement numerous times, I was more convinced than ever that the 'insanity' of Maggie Thatcher meant that the only hook on which we could hang our coats was our original strategy: let Joe McDonnell go to the brink, but by all means possible ensure that he would not die.

I put out a press release in response to Atkins's statement. In it, on behalf of the prisoners, I said that we saw nothing of value in what the Northern Secretary had to say and reiterated our commitment to the five demands, reaffirming that the hunger strike would continue until these were implemented. In the psychological battle that was under way, we had to show that we could be as tough as the British, even though we were reeling from the tone of their statement.

I remember that, on the night of Atkins's statement, anxious comms were being exchanged between Bik, Jake Jackson, Pat Mullin and myself. The statement was a wake-up call that forced us to look into the future with our eyes wide open. We came to the point where we saw little hope in the situation, believing that we were facing a foe who was impervious to our comrades' deaths. I conveyed my own reading of all this to Bik in no uncertain terms. He too knew just how catastrophic Joe McDonnell's death would be. He seemed to be convinced that we should end the hunger strike, come what may.

In a further comm to Adams the next day, Bik pulled

back to our original baseline position. From a situation in which 'Joe is a cert to die', he had swung to a position of telling Adams:

> If this development [the Commission's intervention] is the major undermining effort we've been expecting and we are not able to combat it, then we should seek a way out of this situation, saving lives and as much face as possible. If it doesn't appear that the Brits will be forthcoming with a feasible settlement, then we should get in before public opinion swings against us, forcing us to halt after say six or seven deaths, which would be a disaster. I do not want the war to suffer any setbacks like public condemnation of the movement.

Even though Bik's position had moved to one of actively seeking an end to the hunger strike, he was again throwing the ball to the outside leadership. He didn't want to end the hunger strike without Army Council approval and was looking to the Council to tell him that the British would not offer us a reasonable settlement. Had Bik heard those words from the Council, I am certain that he would have called an end to the hunger strike.

The psychological turmoil that afflicted Bik – and all of us – was immeasurable. But he in particular was carrying a huge burden, a burden that few, if any, republicans had carried before. I believe that he was caught between two poles: his innate humanity told him that we had to face up to the reality that a force mightier than us had defeated us and that the hunger strike should be ended. But that meant that four of our comrades would have died without us achieving our demands. On the other hand, holding the line and maintaining the hunger strike provided a semblance of hope – but almost certainly meant that more comrades would die. Thence Bik's oscillation from a protracted hunger strike to calling the whole thing off as soon as possible.

As a result of the Atkins statement, I concluded that we needed to infuse some realism into the situation. In particular, we had to give the British a way out. I suggested to Bik that we put out a statement to explain our five demands. I advised him that this statement would have to be placatory, even if it still encompassed the substance of our demands. Bik agreed and I set about the task.

We had already determined that any concessions made by the British would apply to all prisoners. Therefore there was nothing to be gained from insisting on the term 'political status' for republican prisoners.

To get around this hurdle, I decided to highlight the fact that we were not elitist and that we would welcome everybody being granted the five demands. The logic of this was that we had already won the broad battle for political status (in the eyes of the world at large, we were political prisoners) by virtue of the fact that four of our number had given their lives for their beliefs. No matter what British government spin doctors might say, they could no longer convince anyone that we were criminally motivated: their 'criminalisation' policy was in shreds.

Although we had decided to drop the terminology, we still wanted the substance. We needed to give the impression that the British government had been misinformed about our five demands, that the five demands could be granted within a liberal prison regime without loss of principle by either party and that the remaining differences could quickly be ironed out, provided the British had the will to settle.

Moreover, we wanted to ensure that segregation from loyalists was brought to the fore. (I would have made that a formal demand at the outset and taken out the insistence on weekly letters, parcels and visits – which 'Ordinary Decent Criminals', or ODCs, already had.) The importance of segregation could not be overstated; there was no guarantee that the British wouldn't try to integrate us at a later date when men were released and our numbers were smaller. In addition, if we had segregation, we would have our own wings and our own power base. Bik and I decided not to use the word 'segregation' in the statement. Instead, we stuck the claim for segregation in with the demand for free association, as if it had been always there.

Bik understood my point of view and supported my position. His talent for public relations was a crucial asset in the statement we eventually wrote. We drafted and redrafted the text, sometimes agonising over a word or sentence for hours until we were happy with it. At last we seemed to be doing something positive – something other than putting men on hunger strike. Bik's contribution was invaluable.

4 JULY STATEMENT

We, the protesting Republican prisoners, having replied in short to H. Atkins' statement of June 30, wish to expand our view of this statement.

1. The British Government are responsible for the hunger strikes in Long Kesh. The ending of special category status was a political tactic used by

the British Government in its attempt to criminalise the Republican attack on British imperialism in Ireland.

The existence of special legislation, special courts and special interrogation, plus the British administration's refusal to acknowledge a special category of prisoners, all contribute to the placing of the responsibility for this issue on the administration's shoulders.

Furthermore, the British Government have had ample opportunities during the course of this issue to avoid the occurrence and recurrence of hunger strikes. The Cardinal Ó Fiaich/NIO talks, and the refusal to honour the 18 December agreement, are prime examples of this.

2. Lord Gardner, like so many other Brit-appointed examiners, was sent to Ireland to do a specific job: to recommend the ending of special category status so that legal credibility could be attached to the criminalisation policy.

3. It is wrong for the British Government to say that we are looking for differential treatment from other prisoners. We would warmly welcome the five demands for all prisoners. Therefore, on this major point of British policy there is no sacrifice of principle involved.

4. We believe that the granting of the five demands to all prisoners would not in any way mean that the administration would be forfeiting control of the prison, nor would their say on prison activities be greatly diminished; but the prisoner could have his dignity restored and cease to occupy the role of establishment zombie.

5. The European Commission on Human Rights

criticised the British Government for being inflexible and for allowing such an impasse to develop. Flexibility is not in perpetuating protest but rather trying to remove or resolve the cause of dissent that foments such protest.

6. Mr Atkins outlined the present work routine under the title 'prison activity'. It is a crude system that Mr Atkins disguises in flowery jargon. Yet, it should not be a major point of contention between the administration and ourselves. What the British Government recognises as 'prison work' we do not. Therefore, with goodwill, 'work' and the achievement of a compatible arrangement should be available without loss of principle. Besides self-education, we are prepared to maintain ourselves, wings, and blocks and engage in any activity which we define as self-maintenance.

7. Mr Atkins is either misinformed or exaggerating the free association demand. Free association means that there would be freedom of movement within the wings. Supervision need not be restricted. That is a matter for the administration's discretion. There would be no interference with prison officers, who would maintain their supervisory role. It must be remembered that the H-Blocks are control units, and each wing is built to accommodate twenty-five prisoners. So it is rather a red herring to speak of the regime losing control of the prison if the prisoners had freedom of movement in the wings.

Equally, it is misleading to quote figures of a hundred prisoners presumably associating together. We believe there should be wing visits but we do not envisage ourselves (although Mr Atkins does) running around the blocks as we please in large numbers.

It is unrealistic to expect Loyalists and Republicans to integrate satisfactorily together. Forced integration, or the deliberate creation of a confrontation between those who bear arms in respect of their highly conflicting political ideologies, is wrong and can only lead to trouble. Even Mr Paisley recognised that fact several years ago.

If studied carefully it will be seen that our definition of free association is far removed from what seems to be Mr Atkins'.

8. Prison clothes are prison clothes. It is illusory to minimise the wearing of prison clothes to half a week. Prisoners, like everyone else, sleep, and for most of the other half are forced to wear prison clothes. The women in Armagh wear their own clothes, and there is no objective reason why all prisoners should not be allowed to wear their own clothes.

9. If we accept that toiletries, and to a lesser extent reading material, are essential, then the weekly parcel amounts to four pounds of fruit. That speaks for itself.

10. Lost remission is a result of the protest and is not connected with the cause of it. As the British Government says, the machinery exists to reclaim it – yet, for some reason, the British Government is being ambiguous on this matter. What constitutes 'subsequent good behaviour'? What does 'one-fifth return of remission' mean?

This should not be an area of disagreement, for it does not directly affect the running of the system. But it is of mutual benefit to all whom it affects that full remission is given back to we prisoners.

Conclusion: In giving our views on what Mr Atkins said, we have outlined what should be the basis of a solution, without loss of principle to either side in this conflict.

It would appear that Mr Atkins has been misinformed about our demands. It certainly appears from his 30 June statement that this is so. We ask all parties to study this statement carefully. We particularly ask the British Government to study it. It should not be taken lightly.

By asking the administration to come in to discuss a resolution, we ask nothing unreasonable. It is common for officials from that administration to visit this prison and converse with prisoners. It has been done before.

Comrades of ours have died and eight of our other comrades presently face death on hunger strike. Our people on the outside have died, and more may die. That is why we seek immediate talks with the British administration to seek a solution to the H-Block protests. It is a reasonable request.

18

The reaction to our statement surpassed all our expectations. While Bik and I hoped that it would open doors that had previously been closed, we couldn't, in our wildest dreams, have anticipated the results of our endeavour. Everyone, from churchmen to politicians, thought it was a major conciliatory statement that showed genuine flexibility and a desire to bring the hunger strike to a negotiated close. Reports in the media said that the British authorities were studying it closely. I was proud of our enterprise. Danny Morrison sent us in a comm stating that it was a 'master stroke' and that it had wrong-footed the British.

Within hours of the statement's release, the British Foreign Office was in contact with the IRA leadership in an effort to reach agreement on the basis of the statement. We heard about this when Bik returned after being summoned to the camp hospital for a visit the next morning – a Sunday, a non-visiting day. Waiting for him was none other than the affable Danny Morrison. (Danny had been banned from the prison since the first hunger strike.) Danny told Bik about the Foreign Office contact and confirmed the contact's bona fides, stating that our outside leadership was certain that he had the endorsement of Thatcher herself. (Gerry Adams is on record as saying that the Foreign Office contact was 'a conduit for the British government with a status above the Northern Ireland secretary of state level' and had been 'authorised at the very highest level'.) This contact, by effortlessly removing the ban on Danny and by getting him into the jail on a Sunday to see our OC and thus implicitly recognising Bik's authority, had sliced through the procedural morass like a hot knife through butter. This development also seemed to vindicate the strategy Bik and I had outlined to Jimmy Teapot, in which we saw Joe McDonnell reaching a critical point at the decisive moment in the hunger strike.

Bik was told that, once again, the contact from the British side was the aptly named 'Mountain Climber'. While we knew him only by his *nom de plume*, we nonetheless assumed that the Mountain Climber was the same individual who had been involved in the first hunger strike. (We later found out that his name was Michael Oatley.) Whoever the Mountain Climber was on this occasion, his mountaineering skills were going to be tested to the full.

There was an agreement that all communications would be treated in the strictest confidence. Both parties knew that our talks circumvented the efforts by the Irish Commission for Justice and Peace and the Irish government to hammer out a settlement and that there would be serious political repercussions if the true nature of what was happening got out. The British regarded this as so important that the Mountain Climber made it clear that the contacts would cease if the link became public knowledge. The method of contact was a direct telephone link between the leadership of the republican movement and the Mountain Climber.

It made perfect sense to me that the British should talk to the Army Council. For a start, doing it that way bypassed all the rigmarole about who should be present at talks in the prison and the 'who could talk to whom' issue that was bedevilling any purposeful dialogue in the jail. Besides, we knew that the Mountain Climber preferred anonymity; given the stark political overtones attached to our negotiating stance, that was understandable. More importantly, why talk to the monkey when you can talk to the organ grinder? In the absence of an IRA Army Convention, the Army Council decided all matters of policy relating to the IRA. The hunger strike was so important to the IRA's struggle that the Army Council's overview would always be crucial in the event of a potential settlement.

Gerry Adams was charged by the Army Council to handle communications with the Mountain Climber. David Beresford, in his book *Ten Men Dead*, describes how:

> Gerry Adams was in a safe house in west Belfast, waiting by the telephone for more messages from the Foreign Office contact, the Mountain Climber.

The coded terminology used in the communications between the Army Council and the British reflected the class system. The British were called 'the management', the Army Council were the 'shop stewards' and the prisoners were 'the workers'. I didn't know about this terminology until years later, but when I did, I couldn't help but remember something my father used to say: 'The workers always get shafted.'

Colm 'Scull' Scullion was more than capable of reading my moods because we had been in a cell together night and day for nearly two years. He had a habit of looking into my face when I was reading Bik's comms. He also knew that Bik being sent for on a Sunday morning was outside the normal course of events. Knowing that he was watching every expression on my face, I tried to be calm as I sat on the mattress reading and rereading Bik's comm. I thought that perhaps it was all going to end soon and that the Brits wanted to settle. Scull's eyes were studiously surveying my face. 'That must be good readin', Rick,' he said.

'It's nothin', Scull.'

'By the look on your face, it doesn't seem like nothin'. For God's sake, what's happenin'?'

'Really, it's nothin'.'

'Is there a deal on the table?'

'Behave yourself. Wouldn't I tell you if there was a deal?'

'Nah, you wouldn't. Fuck sake, Ó Rathaigh, what's goin on?'

'Nothin', Scull!'

'Bollocks! Your eyebrows are dancin'.'

'Seriously, nothin' is happenin'.'

'Why was Bik called to the camp hospital then?'

''Cause the hunger strikers sent for him.'

'Why?'

''Cause Joe was very sick.'

'Aye, dead on. In the name of Jakers, Ó Rathaigh, you know you can tell me. I swear on my mother's life I'll not say a word.'

'Nothing is happenin'.'

'Is the deal done an' dusted? Just nod your head; you don't have to say anythin'.'

'There's no deal done. Settle yourself.'

'You're a bastard, Ó Rathaigh.'

'Nothin's goin' on, Scull.'

Try as he may, Scull wasn't going to get anywhere with his questioning. The IRA operates on a need-to-know basis, and Scull didn't need to know.

In the comm that Bik sent me on his return from the prison hospital, during which he outlined the nature of the contact, he also presented me with a set of British proposals which had emanated from the Mountain Climber. He asked me to give him my opinion on what was on offer from the British. I was amazed at what they were offering. (These concessions are outlined in David Beresford's book *Ten Men Dead* as the essence of what Gerry Adams believed was on offer from the Mountain Climber during the round of negotiations that started after the release of 4 July statement.)

1. All prisoners in Northern Ireland would have the right to have their own clothes at all times as soon as the hunger strike ended.

The way I saw it, it didn't matter whom the British government gave their own clothes to because we had no influence over them in this matter. But through protest and the deaths of our four comrades, the prisoners had forced them to concede on this, the most crucial of the five demands. To anyone with the least knowledge of the situation, having the right to wear our own clothes, or rather not having to wear the 'badge of criminality', the prison uniform, was the critical element in determining who won this confrontation – and the conflict was all about public perception. While achieving favourable prison conditions was desirable to the Blanketmen, the blanket protest hadn't been about prison conditions *per se*; rather, the protest was seen by us as a barricade against a British-government policy that was aimed at depicting the liberation struggle as a huge criminal conspiracy. Republicans wearing the 'monkey suit' would have been the successful manifestation of that policy. Therefore, in terms of the propaganda battle, with our own clothes on our backs we could rightfully claim to have comprehensively defeated the Thatcher government, and that would have translated into a huge morale and propaganda boost for the republican movement.

2. Work would involve self-maintenance activity such as cleaning our cells, wings and blocks, doing our own cooking in the cookhouse, washing our own clothes and generally looking after ourselves. A vague suggestion was made that we should be prepared to build a Catholic chapel in the grounds of the jail.

Most importantly, education was to be recognised as work. In our statement, we had made it clear that what we wanted was self-education, but I could live with our boys attending organised tutorial education – studying for A Levels and the Open University. This was a major policy shift for the regime. Parallel with this, we could educate ourselves whenever we wanted in this new regime (but our self-education would have been of the IRA kind, the education of ideology, as well as in bomb-making and other military matters). In fact, self-education, as Bik and I knew, was a disguise for doing no prison work whatsoever.

What was really significant was that prison work, such as compulsory attendance at workshops, was off the agenda. I surmised that this didn't mean that it was ruled out altogether, but I was confident that, if it was introduced, we could easily make it an untenable proposition through acts of sabotage and disruption. Further, I felt that the British knew us well enough to understand that we had the potential to destroy the prison workshops – and that we would vigorously assert that potential. Most important of all, by offering us this package, the British were signalling their eagerness to leave their baleful problem in Long Kesh behind them. So I thought it unlikely that they would risk resurrecting the spectre of jail protest by attempting to force us into workshops.

3. On free association, there was little movement. Free association was understood by the protesting prisoners to mean that our cell doors would remain open all day until lock-up at 8 PM and that we would be able to move freely within our wings without impediment from the screws. The British had seen through the rhetoric in our statement and realised that to let us have the freedom of the wings all day would certainly lead to us running that part of the jail in which we were housed. Crucially, however, segregation was on offer, and that would have facilitated the command-and-control structure that we needed to exercise our authority over any post-hunger-strike arrangement.

4. Parcels, letters and visits already existed for conforming prisoners, so this wasn't a contentious issue for us. Whether or not we got meat and groceries in a parcel didn't enter into my calculations. There would have been a certain irony in hunger-striking for more food.

5. Half-remission was to be given back on the ending of the hunger strike (although Gerry Adams told the hunger strikers on 29 July that one-fifth was what was being offered; perhaps I picked this up wrong). As I said previously, remission is time taken off one's sentence for

good behaviour. In the North of Ireland, all conforming prisoners, provided they didn't break prison rules, could look forward to having to do only half the time that the judge had sentenced them to. In our case, every day that we spent on the blanket protest was a day lost in remission, a day more that we would have to spend in prison. Some Blanketmen had lost over four years' remission and were the government to give a half, or a fifth for that matter, of that lost remission back, many would have been released straight away. Again, remission, like correspondence, visits and parcels, wasn't high on my list of priorities. While it was important in the long term, it wasn't a core demand and therefore, in my view, was incidental to an overall settlement. The substance of political status and our ability to claim the propaganda victory was all that concerned me. We had hardly risked our liberty in a freedom struggle to win remission from prison.

My first reaction was one of astonishment. I read the comm that Bik had sent up over and over again in case I had got it wrong. What I was reading was astounding. It seemed that the underlying substance of our demands was being conceded to us.

The only core demand on which there had been little movement was free association. Its absence was a considerable, although not insurmountable, setback, in my opinion, and I spent a long time debating with myself the consequences of entering a post-hunger-strike era without free association having been achieved. In the end, I concluded that, while this was more than a peripheral demand, it certainly was not as important as the clothes and the prison-work issues. The fact that segregation was on offer convinced me that, come what may, as soon as 'the doors were open' and we were off the protest, we would be the bosses in our own wings, and God help the screw who tried to control us. I could live with the prospect of having a screw stand at the top of the wing and being banged up during a few set breaks during the day, if the option was to end the hunger strike with nothing or to continue into a protracted strike. We could allow for slack because, ultimately, segregation would mitigate any detrimental effects that might arise from the absence of full free association.

Did these concessions go far enough? Was the glass half-empty or half-full? I thought it was three-quarters full. In fact, the British had gone further than I had considered possible: I felt it was almost too good to be true. I asked myself how the British government would sell this in Westminster. But that was hardly our problem: the proposals were there in black and white, direct from Thatcher's desk.

I thought that the offer was sufficient for us to settle the dispute honourably. As I saw it, the offer from the Mountain Climber had reduced the gap between his bottom line and our maximum demands to the point where it wasn't then worth more comrades dying.

I was acutely aware that, should Joe McDonnell die (he was only four or five days, at the most, away from dying), we would be in a different and more dangerous phase of the hunger strike. Like us, the British would see his death as the crossing of a threshold and would then probably dig in for the long haul. There was another important consideration: by not taking what was on offer, we ran the risk of the British removing it from the table altogether.

After about three hours spent arguing with myself

over the pros and cons of the Mountain Climber's offer, I reached the conclusion that, in all conscience, these proposals formed the basis of a honourable settlement. I called Bik up to the window (our conversation was conducted in Irish).

'Well, Rick?' he asked.

'I think there's enough there, Bikso.'

'I agree. I'll write to the outside an' let them know our thinkin'.'

The boys in the wing picked up on these words and realised their significance. There was an immediate mood of exuberance as men who had been sullen and downcast began talking to each other out of their cell windows.

I was euphoric: it seemed to me that Bobby, Frank, Raymond and Patsy's huge sacrifice had broken the British government – something I hadn't thought possible. No more hunger strikers would have to die for their beliefs. All that was left was for the Army Council to rubber-stamp our acceptance of the deal – a matter that Bik and I both considered would be a formality, given that we appeared to have won four of our five demands.

As well as negotiating with the Mountain Climber, Gerry Adams was busy trying to get the Commission for Justice and Peace to throw in the towel. The commission was now, without knowing it, undermining matters by advocating a deal which, on the face of it, seemed to offer more than the Mountain Climber was prepared to offer. And there was no evidence that what the commission believed was on offer had the backing of the British government.

In an attempt to advance things, and in the hope of eliciting a positive response from the British, the commission was, on 6 July, preparing a summary of what it believed it had agreed with the British government.

The fact that the British hadn't indicated to us, publicly or privately, that they had reached an agreement with the commission suggested that there was no common ground between the parties. Therefore the commission's statement would put pressure on the British by forcing them either to deny or to verify that they and the commission had reached an agreed position. What if the British government didn't agree with the commission's interpretation of what the commission thought was on offer? That could jeopardise the Mountain Climber's initiative by forcing the government to adopt an even stronger stance in public than it had in private. And if a dispute arose between the commission and the government, there would be little room for retreat. Therefore, the best option appeared to be to tell the commission of the Mountain Climber's initiative and what was really on offer, in the hope that this would persuade the commission to withdraw from the field and leave matters to the British government and the IRA Army Council.

Against this backdrop, Adams sent word to the commission that he wanted to see its members. They met in a house in Andersonstown, in west Belfast. Father Oliver Crilly and Hugh Logue represented the commission, and Adams briefed them on the Mountain Climber's offer. Hugh Logue told Padraig O'Malley, the author of the hunger-strike book *Biting at the Grave*, that Adams 'had in minute detail all the concessions we were being offered and we didn't doubt that he was in contact with them [the British]'.

The commission postponed its press conference and hurriedly left for Stormont Castle to confront the minister of state responsible for prisons, Michael Allison, about Adams's disclosure. Allison was said to be 'nonplussed' at the revelation, convincing the commission members that he was genuinely in the dark.

Given the history of contacts between the IRA and successive British governments, the commission should have at least suspected that the British were more than capable of opening a separate dialogue with the IRA. In the winter of 1972, Howard Smith, the UK co-ordinator of intelligence between the RUC, the British army and the intelligence services, met with leading republicans Ruairí Ó Bradaigh and Dáithí Ó Conaill in Ballsbridge, Dublin, to discuss conditions for a truce. On 13 March 1972, the then British Prime Minister, Harold Wilson, met secretly with the IRA in Ó Conaill's house in Dublin. In June 1972, the Conservative Secretary of State for Northern Ireland, Willie Whitelaw, twice met an IRA delegation in London. British officials repeatedly met the IRA during the 1975 ceasefire. Now, a representative of the British government (the Mountain Climber) was talking (through an intermediary) to the IRA during the first hunger strike. The commission must have known about these contacts, given the make-up of their panel. They would have been very naïve not to suspect that something might be happening between the two principal parties, far removed from the glare of the television cameras.

19

If we thought the response from the Army Council would be a formality and that, like us, its members would accept the British offer, we were to be sadly mistaken. On the afternoon of 6 July, a comm came in from the Army Council saying that it did not think that the Mountain Climber's proposals provided the basis for a resolution and that more was needed. The message said that the right to free association was vital to an overall settlement and that its exclusion from the proposals, along with ambiguity on the issue of what constituted prison work, made the deal unacceptable. The Council was hopeful, though, that the Mountain Climber could be pushed into making further concessions. As usual, the comm had come from Gerry Adams, who had taken on the unenviable role of transmitting the Army Council's views to the prison leadership.

Bik and I were shattered. The possibility that the Council might reject the proposals had never entered into our calculations. We were convinced that we had achieved a great victory and that the republican movement could present the deal as a momentous triumph; now it appeared that our analysis and optimism had been both flawed and premature. At the time, I believed that the leadership felt we had jumped at the first available set of proposals and clumsily accepted them, when, as stated by the Army Council, a second and better offer might come from the Mountain Climber.

The Mountain Climber's hat was still in the ring, so the negotiating process remained alive. We asked ourselves why the Mountain Climber would keep the channel open if there wasn't room for manoeuvre? Surely if this was an on-off offer, his best tactic would have been to heap pressure on us by presenting us with an ultimatum and giving us a deadline to either accept or reject the offer, under threat of closing down the channel? So there was still a fight to be fought. But as the shifting rays of moonlight on the wall of the cell reminded me, time was not on our side: the fire of life in Joe McDonnell was close to being extinguished.

Bik and I spoke quietly at the window (we were only two cells apart), but there wasn't much we could say. I don't know how he felt, but at that moment, I felt like a rank amateur.

It needs to be understood that Bik and I attributed almost godlike status to the IRA leadership. They alone had first identified the British super-plan of Ulster-isation, criminalisation and normalisation, when the rest of us were engrossed in ceasefires and feuding. It was they who had replaced the old regime, which had been responsible for those disastrous policies, and, with the introduction of the cell structure and the long-war strategy, had rescued the struggle from defeat. In the light of these achievements, we believed that their analysis of our opinion was justified because we thought that, tactically, they were far superior to us.

As the situation moved beyond our control, it became evident that the real power in the republican movement was asserting its authority. This time, the 'shop stewards', not the 'management', had consigned the prison leadership to the role of 'workers' in the general scheme of things, and the 'shop stewards' and the 'management' were going to sort things out – no matter what the 'workers' thought.

While I was convinced that our Army Council believed that we had acted prematurely when we accepted the offer and that a second, better offer could materialise, I nonetheless harboured doubts about the wisdom of their tactics. What if the second offer didn't come? There would then be no escaping the fact that we would be into a protracted hunger strike, and there was no telling how many hunger strikers would eventually die. From where I stood, it appeared that both the 'management' and the 'shop stewards' were about to engage in brinkmanship. But brinkmanship is a dangerous game, and I asked myself if it was wise for our leadership to endanger the life of Joe McDonnell – and God knows how many others who were queuing up behind him – over whether we were banged up for a couple of hours during the day.

While Adams and those close to him continued with their secret negotiations, Bik, and the few of us who were privy to the Mountain Climber's initiative, waited for the breakthrough, entreating God for deliverance and hoping.

In reply to the Army Council comm rejecting the proposals, Bik wrote to Adams on 6 July: 'I sincerely hope you have been successful in all your efforts . . . I'm hoping and praying that we all do the right thing.' It was a prayer I shared.

On the evening of 6 July, Bik wrote to Adams again. While he did not censure the Army Council, it was clear that he had serious doubts about rejecting the Mountain Climber's proposals:

> I don't know if you've thought of this line, but I have been thinking that if we don't pull this off and Joe dies, then the 'RA are going to come under some bad stick from all quarters. Everybody is crying the place down that a settlement is there and those commission chappies are convinced that they have breached Brit principles. Anyway we'll sit tight and see what comes.

Bik was as enthusiastic as I was about the Mountain Climber's proposals. He wanted the hunger strike stopped and hoped that a sympathetic ear would heed his plea. It wasn't the first time that he had put out feelers about ending the hunger strike – nor was it the first time that his words had fallen on deaf ears. Less than two weeks earlier, he had written to Adams to say that we might have to accept the Commission's proposals:

> If this development [the commission's intervention] is the major undermining effort we've been expecting and we are not able to combat it, then we should seek a way out of this situation, saving lives and as much face as possible.

With the Mountain Climber's offer, we didn't need to combat the commission's intervention because we believed that that body was now out of the frame. We were in direct talks with the British government, we had a solid package on offer direct from the British and the prison leadership had accepted it. Bik had also said back then:

If it doesn't appear that the Brits will be forth-coming with a feasible settlement, then we should get in before public opinion swings against us, forcing us to halt after say six or seven deaths, which would be a disaster.

Before Bik's 7 July comm reached Adams, Joe McDonnell was dead. He died at 4.50 AM on the sixty-sixth day of his hunger strike. He was thirty years old. He had two children, eleven-year-old Joseph and ten-year-old Bernadette.

Less than three hours after Joe died, sixteen-year-old John Dempsey, a member of Na Fianna Éireann, the youth wing of the republican movement, was shot dead by British security forces at the Falls Road bus depot. It was alleged by soldiers at the time that he was preparing to throw an unlit petrol bomb at one of them. The next day, fifteen-year-old Danny Barrett was shot dead by members of the British army in the Ardoyne area while sitting on his garden wall. Also on that day, thirty-three-year-old Nora McCabe was killed by a plastic bullet fired from an RUC Land Rover. It was accepted at her inquest that Mrs McCabe had left her sister's house in Linden Street, Falls Road, to get cigarettes and had not been involved in any disturbance.

On the day that Joe died, a comm came in from Adams to say that he had been by the telephone all night awaiting a call from the Mountain Climber, anticipating that it would contain the vital second offer. But in Adams's express opinion, the Mountain Climber had been under the assumption that Joe had had a few more days left in him (an assumption we shared) and had delayed making the crucial second offer, preferring to take matters to the wire in a battle of nerves. We all knew from experience that, if the British were to blink at all, it would be immediately before Joe drew his last breath, and if he died, their tactics would be aimed at shifting the moral responsibility for his death onto us.

On the morning of Joe's death, 8 July 1981, Bik sent Adams a further comm:

> Comrade Mór, got your comm today alright. I was wrecked when I read it. The whole thing could have been settled now. You must be worn out *cara*. I know that what happened surprised the Brits. I sat here this morning and cursed them to high heavens. I had a good idea they were operating every bloody angle to outflank us some way and take Joe to the brink.

Later that day, Bik sent Adams yet another comm, telling him that he had visited the hunger strikers.

> Pennies [Danny Morrison] had already informed them [the hunger strikers] of the Mountain Climber angle and they accepted this one hundred percent. They accept the view that the Brits, in trying to play us too close to the line, made a blunder and didn't reckon on Joe dying.

I was in agreement with Bik's assessment, yet in the hard light of day there is no evidence whatsoever to substantiate that a second offer would ever be made. On the contrary, as events later proved during the second bout of negotiations with the Mountain Climber, which began eleven days after Joe died, the British government's base offer was their only offer.

It is hard to escape from the probability that, rather than the British officials mistiming Joe's death, the republican decision-makers were intent on washing their hands of any culpability in Joe's death, given our acceptance of the deal. But what else could they have done? They could hardly have owned up to the charge of having ridden roughshod over the prisoners' wish to settle. This would have resulted in massive political fallout amongst republicans and nationalists throughout Ireland and abroad. Undoubtedly, a hostile press would have levelled the charge that the republican leadership, by ignoring the prisoners' desire to take the deal, had brought about the death of Joe McDonnell and any hunger strikers who died after him.

A generous interpretation of the second-offer theory would be that the Army Council, or those charged by them with overseeing the hunger strike, disastrously miscalculated on all fronts. A more sceptical view would be that perhaps they didn't miscalculate at all: perhaps getting a republican elected in Bobby's former constituency of Fermanagh/South Tyrone and thus kick-starting the shift away from armed struggle and into constitutional politics was the real reason they baulked at accepting what appeared to be a very sellable deal. If that were so, Joe and the five other hunger strikers who died after him were used as cannon fodder. No matter which way one views it, the outside leadership alone, not the prison leadership, took the decision to play brinkmanship with Joe McDonnell's life. If Bik and I had had our way, Joe and the five comrades who followed him to the grave would be alive today.

In the H-Blocks, we didn't question the Army Council's belief in the second offer. As far as Bik and I were concerned at this time, their negotiating tactics had a bedrock of hard logic about them, and we both agreed that, in the end, they had been thwarted by bad luck. Therefore there was no reason to doubt the Army Council's view that the British government had been at fault. Given our blind faith in the leadership, it was always easier to blame the British if something went wrong.

Joe's death was a demoralising blow for me, not only because I had known him since 1972, when we were on the *Maidstone* together, and counted him as a good friend, but also because I had been uneasy about our Army Council adopting its second-offer strategy. I had come to the conclusion that, in the wake of Humphrey Atkins's inflexible statement of 29 June, we needed to give the British government a way out. I had been the inspiration behind, and the primary architect of, the ground-breaking 4 July statement. That statement had opened the door to the Mountain Climber's offer. Now that door had been closed, albeit temporarily (although we weren't to know that at the time). No matter how I tried to rationalise it, I felt that the difference between our maximum demands and what was on offer did not warrant Joe's life, or those of his fellow hunger strikers, being put at risk in the first place.

After Joe's death, the line of communication with the British government went dead. That was a black period for us. Various questions gripped us – and scared the life out of us. Would we ever hear from the Mountain Climber again? And if he came back to the negotiating table, would he improve on his previous offer? In moments of deep despair, I found myself staring vacantly at a world that had turned into a dark and frightening place. We were on the wrong side of a

Rubicon that we had promised never to cross. And we had crossed it, even though we had been offered a way to avoid doing so!

The Irish Commission for Justice and Peace released its statement on the day Joe McDonnell died, amid confusion and bitter recrimination between the commission and the Northern Ireland Office. The statement contained what the commission believed had been agreed – on the face of it much more than the Mountain Climber was offering – even though Hugh Logue believed that Adams's explanation of the Mountain Climber's offer contained exactly what the commission was convinced it had secured.

The commission believed that it had secured a measure of free association and less lock-up time than the Mountain Climber was offering. There were also subtle differences, to our advantage, between the commission's proposed work regime and what was in the Mountain Climber's proposals.

The commission also said that an NIO official was due to visit the hunger strikers to explain the fine print of the proposals. The NIO apparently agreed to send in an official, but the prison medical staff assured them that Joe had a couple of days to live; they therefore procrastinated. In the aftermath of Joe's death, the NIO official went into the prison, but he merely repeated the same old rigmarole that nothing was on offer.

The commission said that it suspected that its members 'were in fact being seriously misled' by the British and ended the statement by criticising the British government for 'clawing back' from their predetermined position. In reply Michael Allison, the minister of state for prisons, said, according to *Ten Men Dead*, that the commission's document was 'wildly euphoric and wildly out of perspective'. Allison alluded to the perception that the commission had taken his 'privately held sentiments' and exaggerated them to give the impression that a solution was near. But, in his own words, 'there was a lady behind the veil' – Margaret Thatcher – and she must have overruled him.

The commission eventually packed up and left the battlefield. Was the commission the Trojan horse that Adams and others believed it to be? There is little doubt that the commission acted in good faith with the British, with the aim of teasing out exactly what we would settle for. In the end, however, there was no proof of a serious British commitment to implement what the commission thought had been agreed. Michael Allison, with whom they believed they were negotiating, did not have the authority to vouchsafe anything.

Allison went on to tell reporters in New York, after Joe McDonnell's death, that 'you [British negotiators] continued talking while you figured out a way to defeat them' – proof that the devil has friends in high places. If this was not a *post hoc* rationalisation to cover himself after being publicly humiliated by Thatcher, it showed that defeating us was the only thing on his mind. Therefore, the commission was being manipulated. Gerry Adams was accurate in his assessment that the British were cynically using the commission for their own ends. The day after Joe McDonnell died, I issued a statement, as requested by the Army Council, condemning the commission for letting the British government influence them.

At this juncture, our train went off the rails, and the strategy of 'no compromise' came into effect, as I had always suspected it would eventually. But 'no compromise' was a euphemism for 'no strategy'; from that point on, emotion, and the frantic desire to prove that our comrades had not died for nothing, shackled everybody. The question that Shakespeare's *Titus Andronicus* posed kept flashing into my mind: 'When will this fearful slumber have an end?'

20

On 13 July, five days after Joe McDonnell's death, Bik, Tom 'Buck' Bradley, Marty McManus, Scull and I were in the washhouse. A screw, Ralphie Gilmore, stood stoically humming to himself and then moved to let Lorny McKeown into the wing. Lorny had been on hunger strike for fifteen days by that stage. As he came through the steel-grille doors at the top of the wing, he hit us with the most shocking news: Martin Hurson was dead.

I looked at Bik and his face turned white, his eyebrows meeting to form a furrowed 'V'. Another screw who was escorting Lorny pushed him, and we all immediately surrounded the screw. Another one of our comrades was dead, and this bastard was pushing a hunger striker around? A confrontation followed, and only an order from Bik saved the screw from the beating of his life.

The shock of Martin's death was enormous. He wasn't even remotely near the danger zone, having been on hunger strike for only forty-six days; it was a mystery why he had died so soon. Eventually, we found out that he had an infection in his stomach and had suffered a most horrific death.

If we had known about his condition in time, we

would have intervened to save his life, but nobody in the prison administration had either the wit or the desire to approach us. Matt Devlin from Martin's native Tyrone replaced him on hunger strike. The death count now stood at six.

Six days later, Father Faul came into our block to say Mass. The canteen was packed with Blanketmen, and the noise was deafening. Father Faul (or 'Denis the Menace', as we called him) walked through the grille door and made straight for the food-serving area, where Bik, Jake Jackson, Pat Mullin and I were standing. Bik nudged me and nodded towards Father Faul, whose face was roaring red.

'You are responsible for the death of Martin Hurson!' he shouted at Bik.

'Gimme that again?' said Bik, physically stiffening.

'You are responsible for Martin Hurson's death, McFarlane.'

There followed the most vicious verbal confrontation between a priest and one of his flock I have ever witnessed, with Father Faul accusing Bik of killing Martin, and Bik shouting back that the British government bore sole responsibility for Hurson-Boy's death. Bik tried to tell Father Faul that we didn't even know that Martin had an infection in his stomach and that, if we had been made aware of that fact, we would have taken him off the hunger strike, but the cleric did not want to listen.

As things heated up, Bik accused Father Faul of undermining and perpetuating the hunger strike and helping the British. Father Faul countered that Bik should go on hunger strike himself and see what it was like. At that stage, Bik began to lose his temper; I had to pull him away because I thought he was going to throw a punch at the cleric.

Bik was badly shaken by the incident, and I had a job cooling him down. The last thing we needed was for such an outrageous allegation to be levelled at any of us. But was there a whispering campaign under way that was starting to point the finger at us, saying that the prison leadership was immune to the suffering that the hunger strike was causing? It was all I could do to keep Bik from joining the hunger strike; Father Faul, although genuinely upset by Martin's death, wasn't helping matters by levelling such accusations.

Pressure had been growing on the families of the surviving hunger strikers to intervene to stop the protest. Father Faul was now saying publicly that the republican movement seemed to be more interested in political gain than in trying to stop the hunger strike and was manipulating the strikers. His view was that, since Maggie Thatcher seemed adamant that she would not grant the five demands, it was wrong to continue the hunger strike. He guessed that the Army Council must surely have reached the same conclusion; his frustration came from its refusal to order it to end.

Father Faul did not know about the Mountain Climber, about the offer he had made or about the prison leadership's acceptance of that offer. Nor did he know that the Army Council had rejected our acceptance. Hell hath no fury like an angry priest: Father Faul would have roasted the Army Council had he been aware of what was really going on.

Despite a huge protest in Dublin on 18 July, during which seventeen Gardaí and fifty protesters were injured, the level of support on the streets in the North was waning, and a settlement seemed further off than ever. Our people were exhausted, and there appeared to be little spirit left in them. I shared their feelings. No one knew more than me how frustrating this process was. The H-Blocks were becoming a killing field, and there was nothing I could do about it. If there had been a way of leaving the hunger strike – but not the hunger strikers – behind, I would have gone for it.

Kevin Lynch and Big Doc (Kieran Doherty) were deteriorating rapidly, and the pressure on us all was awesome. My thoughts constantly turned to them. I remembered Kevin's irrepressible *joie de vivre* and his amiable Dungiven mannerisms. He was a lovely person. And I could still see Big Doc, a fantastic Gaelic footballer, fielding a high ball as he played alongside me when we had been interned in Cage 3 together. He had such vigour and strength then as he effortlessly brushed aside crunching tackles; now he was facing the extinction of his life-force. My mind would have turned to the other lads in the camp hospital, but that only led to gut-wrenching feelings of helplessness, inadequacy and guilt. How could I, who was going to emerge from this feverish plague with my life intact, with a future that would eventually extend beyond my prison cell, even begin to understand their anguish? Did the prospect of dying terrify them, or was death to be welcomed as a liberation from their pain? Lorny McKeown, as he approached the end of his hunger strike, described very vividly how he saw his coming death:

I knew that I had now no more than two days left to live, if even that, but I was too tired to dwell on that thought. In fact, in many ways it [death] appeared inviting, more or less as a release.

When I read Lorny's account of his hunger strike in *Nor Meekly Serve My Time*, I was deeply moved at the spirit of the man, even more so when he wrote about a visit by a camp doctor, who told him:

> These purple marks on your chest and arms are blood vessels which have broken down and collapsed. Your sight has been permanently damaged. Your vital organs are under intense strain at the moment. There are a number of ways you will die: your kidneys or liver could collapse at any moment. Either way, you can expect to die very shortly.

On the day of the confrontation between Father Faul and Bik, 19 July, the British Foreign Office reactivated the Mountain Climber initiative. Their motive, we believed, was to assuage the international criticism that was almost certain to be directed against Thatcher at the upcoming Western Leaders Summit in Ottawa. The next day, we were told that the talks were on again.

A comm came in from Adams saying that the British seemed to be more focused on trying to get a resolution but that lack of clarity on prison work and a point-blank refusal by them to consider the free-association demand were still stumbling blocks. As a result of that upbeat comm, a discussion began about who could guarantee a deal between the British and ourselves. Bik and Jake Jackson spent quite a bit of time on this issue. The name of Lord Carrington, the former British foreign minister, was thrown into the ring as an honest broker. I didn't get too involved. In fact, it was a bit bizarre because, here we were, after six men had died, only now starting to consider guarantors – and who do we come up with but a former British Tory minister!

Another comm came in from Adams on 22 July, stating that talks with the Mountain Climber had broken down once more and that nothing new was on offer. Adams outlined the Army Council's view that we were facing two options: to end the hunger strike immediately without accepting the Mountain Climber's proposals or to stay on hunger strike, basically hope for the best and pray that at some time in the future the British government would concede to our five demands. He then repeated the Army Council's opinion that the Mountain Climber's proposals did not provide the basis for an honourable settlement. The reason given was that the Council thought that there was too much distance between the Mountain Climber's offer and what was needed to validate the deaths of the six hunger strikers. By presenting us with only two choices, the Army Council was stating clearly that only implementation of the full five demands, in their entirety, was now sufficient to bring an end to the hunger strike.

Adams also contended that, if the prisoners opted to continue with the hunger-strike strategy, there was no telling how many men would die. He made no bones about the fact that there was no guarantee that the British would eventually cave in. At no time did he suggest or advise that we stay on hunger strike, but neither did he advocate ending the strike. Instead, he left the decision to the prison leadership and to those on hunger strike.

Adams also said that the republican movement would respect any decision we made, adding that no damage would be done to the movement if we decided to end the strike. He said that he believed that the Mountain Climber was being honest with him and described the last communication from the British as a 'very frank statement' which outlined their policy position. That 'very frank' statement reinforced the British belief that it was impossible for them to concede the full five demands, even if they had wanted to.

The rub, however, was that Adams also said that the Mountain Climber had indicated that he was sad that it had come to this and had informed Adams that, at some time in the future, circumstances might change and the British government might be forced to go further, 'but no politician in England could afford to gamble his political future on that assumption', the Mountain Climber had told Adams.

Bik and I both knew the consequences of what was being proposed, and there was little for us to discuss. Distraught to the point of desolation, I shut down and crawled under the blankets. But while it may be possible to shut down the body, it is not so easy to shut down a brain that is used to racing at high speed. What distraction would give me comfort from the trauma that assaulted me like giant hailstones every second of every day? I tried to think of Bernie and my daughter, but somehow they seemed to be distant figures. Scull was sitting on his bed across from me; he knew that my foul mood augured ill. He kept asking me what was wrong, but I couldn't bring myself even to mutter a reply, and so I turned towards the wall. The names of birds in Irish were written on the wall; strikingly, there was Bobby's favourite bird, the lark, or *fuiseóg*. There were always reminders; there was no escape. I was freezing. Scull lent me a blanket. I closed my eyes and prayed that I would wake up and find that my friends weren't dead after all and that this most devilish of all dreams was only a nightmare. Alas, trying to tread softly on dreams is the preserve of poets and philosophers.

My assessment of the latest Adams comm was that this was now patently a lose-lose situation for us. His first option – ending the hunger strike without accepting the deal – meant that we would be back to square one, but six of our comrades would have died for nothing. The second option was to continue with the hunger strike and hope for the best – which basically meant that the remaining eight hunger strikers in the camp hospital, and possibly more, were likely to follow them! The more I looked at it, the more I realised that what Adams was saying was that only the full five demands would be enough for the Army Council to countenance advising, or ordering, an end to the hunger strike. That being the case, there was effectively only one course of action open to us, and that was to continue with the hunger strike and hope against hope, as the Mountain Climber had said, that circumstances might change and the British government would somehow go further. To end the hunger strike now with nothing, and for those six comrades to have died in vain, was inconceivable.

In the grand scheme of things, I felt that there was more than a touch of the Pontius Pilate about Adams's latest comm. It was clear that the IRA had decided on what was and was not a resolution and had overruled us when we had wanted to settle. That had effectively consigned the prison leadership to bit-players in a stage-managed production where nobody wanted a credit. Yet while they were doing this, other republicans were telling the nationalist people of Belfast, Derry, Tyrone, south Armagh and elsewhere that we alone were running the show, that they had little or no influence over us and that we were hell-bent on attaining the five demands in their totality – irrespective of how many lives were lost. Omission, rather than lies, was the order of the day: the leadership never told the hunger strikers' relatives of the Mountain Climber's intervention and they washed their hands of any responsibility for making or breaking the deal. Years later, Peter Taylor, in his book *Provos*, asked the question: 'Why was the hunger strike not settled once six men had died and the substance of the five demands seemed to be on offer?' Taylor, like others, misses the point. His question should have been: why was the hunger strike not settled once *four* men had died and the substance of the five demands seemed to be on offer?

The offer hadn't changed; it might have been more placatory in tone, but the fundamentals remained the same. A serious and objective reading of *Ten Men Dead* throws up all sorts of contradictions. Who rejected the first Mountain Climber offer? Who dictated the two-option line? It wasn't the prisoners.

Adams's comm amounted to us being cut adrift in the Roaring Forties in a little dingy that had been holed below the waterline. Only the full five demands would suffice? That was a fate-sealing, doom-laden edict. The fact was that the Army Council was now returning the decision-making process to us in Long Kesh – as long as we didn't take the only feasible route out of those troubled waters: to accept the Mountain Climber's offer. But in the end, it was responsibility, rather than power, which had shifted.

Bik replied to that 'two-option' comm on the same day, accepting Adams's view:

I fully agree with the two options you outlined. It is either a settlement or it isn't. No room for half-measures or meaningless cosmetic exercises. Better be straight about it and just come out and say *sin é* – no more!!

But Bik was incapable of saying '*sin é*'. We all were! By throwing in the towel, we would have been admitting that we had been devastatingly defeated, no matter what gloss we put on it. Not only that but, critically, six valiant comrades, all in the prime of life, were dead, and they were looking over our shoulders as well as the hunger strikers'.

In relation to the British government's belief that it was beyond their power to deliver the five demands, Bik said: 'It is something we had already known (or at least suspected).' Here, Bik is only reaffirming his and my own position during the initial debate on 20 December 1980, when we both questioned the rationale behind the hunger-strike tactic. Having acknowledged our limit-ations, Bik, later in that comm to Adams, said: 'It is we who are on top of the situation and we who are stronger. Therefore we maintain.'

The confusion and contradictions in Bik's reply to Adams were shared by us all. None of us knew where to go next, other than to stick to the hunger strike and pray that a breakthrough would come. More than anything, we had to demonstrate publicly, as well as in private, our absolute loyalty to and faith in the Army Council.

In that comm, Bik also made it clear that he didn't know exactly what it was he was rejecting in the second Mountain Climber negotiations: 'You can give me a rundown on exactly how far the Brits went,' he wrote.

By the time Bik eventually heard the fine detail of the

second proposals, the Mountain Climber had returned to base camp. The climb was over; the mountain had proved to be unclimbable.

What is obvious in hindsight is that the prison leadership was too emotionally dysfunctional to countenance ending the hunger strike. Where was our outside leadership when we needed it most?

I was asking myself, again and again (and I remember the exact words): 'What the fuck am I doin' in the middle of this? Why isn't someone more experienced than me doin' this bastard of a job?' I felt like punching the walls in frustration. Dead men may have been looking over my shoulder, but live hunger strikers, men who would soon be dead, were effectively looking into my face, and I was turning my head away. I knew in the depths of my being that our cause was lost and I was allowing myself to drift with the current. Since that time, I have had to grapple with the terrible knowledge that I personally displayed an appalling degree of moral ambivalence on the issue of the hunger strike. I let my hunger-striking comrades down; I took the line of least resistance rather than say the unpalatable words that no one wanted to hear. In fact, it wasn't until the tenth man had died that I wrote Bik a comm telling him that both The Dark and I believed that we should end the hunger strike.

Jimmy Teapot, who did not know about the Mountain Climber, had sensed weeks before Joe McDonnell's death that the five demands were beyond our reach. Seanna Walsh, the camp adjutant (who was second in command to the OC and who played little part in the running of the hunger strike because he was in another block), took his name off the hunger-strike list because, in his view:

As we keep pushing forward, it [the hunger strike] keeps getting bigger and bigger. However, the problem for us is that we are pushing it uphill and the danger facing us is, if we take the pressure off, it runs back again and crushes us all. So far the Brits had taken everything we could throw at them. At some stage the people are going to see it as our responsibility to end the hunger strike and all that pressure is going to come back on us . . . I withdrew my name from the list of volunteers for hunger strike. I no longer felt that we would be dying for 'political status' or for the struggle, but we would be dying because we couldn't let Bobby, Francie, Patsy, Raymond, Joe and Martin down.

Despite this very rational position, Seanna, to my knowledge, did not call on Bik to end the hunger strike.

21

Bik sent me a comm saying that he was again seriously considering going on hunger strike himself. He asked, almost begged, me to come up with a form of words that would convince the leadership to allow him to join the hunger strike. In retrospect, I am convinced that Bik saw how impossible his role had become, and I think he simply wanted to escape from the situation. The best – indeed only – escape route for him was to go on hunger strike himself.

There were tactical gains to be made in Bik going on hunger strike. For a start, it would remove the perennial problem of the British authorities not recognising or talking to camp staff. They were prepared to talk directly to hunger strikers, and if Bik was a hunger striker, he could effectively negotiate with them without them feeling that they had conceded on recognition.

Armed with the Mountain Climber's 'frank statement', however, I felt that there was little or no point in that; the British government wasn't prepared to go beyond what they had originally proposed. I told Bik that, in my opinion, there was nothing to be gained from his going on hunger strike.

If Bik wasn't in complete psychological disarray, I certainly was. The 4 July statement had been my best shot at trying to end the hunger strike, and it hadn't succeeded. I concluded that no amount of clever prose on my part could turn this around; we could not win this battle.

Bobby and those who had followed him had embarked on the hunger strike in pessimistic frames of mind, but I think that their human nature would have entertained a sliver of hope that there could be a life before death and that a settlement with honour would be found before they died. Unfortunately, that possibility had come and gone. I shared Seanna Walsh's opinion when he said: 'I no longer felt that they [the hunger strikers] would be dying for "political status".'

I was plagued by feelings of guilt, which came with the shattering burden of having helped Bik vet potential hunger strikers. I lay awake at night thinking about how good republicans and friends, whom we had selected, would receive the Army Council comm that told them they would be going on hunger strike at a prearranged time. I cringed at the role I had played in the selection process; 'death process' was nearer to the mark, I thought.

Unlike Bik, though, I hadn't the consolation of knowing that I had put my name down for the hunger strike. My hesitation to stand shoulder to shoulder with my hunger-striking comrades left me in emotional upheaval. This incongruity clashed with everything I had been taught by my deceased OC, Jim Bryson. Bryson, of whom I had been a willing disciple, had instilled in his Volunteers the ethos that leaders should always be the first to climb the ladder and lead their troops over the top. Not for him the safety of the palatial *château*, ten miles behind the trenches. My cell may not have been a *château*, but it was certainly miles behind the trenches, and that knowledge gnawed at my soul.

I knew that Bernie would never be able to understand why I would want to volunteer for the hunger strike. How *could* she comprehend my chain of thought? I could hardly make sense of it myself.

Despite all this, I could no longer sit back, so I put my name forward for the hunger strike. Once again, I selfishly took the easy way out: I decided that it was best not to tell Bernie the news until I got word that I had been selected.

I got a taste of what to expect if she should hear the news when I had a visit with her shortly after I had volunteered for the hunger strike. During the visit I spoke of nothing but the fast and the political development of the republican movement. On top of that, it had been arranged that I was to give my next monthly visit to a leading French trade unionist to brief her on the hunger strike. Bernie cracked up on hearing that: 'A French trade unionist? You're goin' to give my only monthly visit to a complete stranger? What about me an' wee Bernadette? Do ya ever consider what we're goin' through, Ricky? It's always you, isn't it?' Try as I may, I couldn't convince her that everyone else in the leadership had made sacrifices in relation to visits and that I had to share the load.

After the visit, she made her way to the Sinn Féin incident centre and delivered a comm to Liam Óg that I had passed to her on the visit. Liam Óg saw the anger in her and asked if she was all right. Her reply was stark: 'All right? Fuck Ricky O'Rawe, fuck the IRA, fuck you an' fuck Maggie Thatcher too.' To his credit, Liam Óg took time out of his busy schedule to listen to her pent-up rage and explained the situation to her better than I could. An enduring friendship was born.

Pat McGeown, or Pat Beag ('Wee Pat'), as we called him, was entering the final stages of his hunger strike in the prison hospital. He was privy to our decision-making process, although I do not know whether or not he knew that Bik and I were positive about the Mountain Climber's offer. Pat Beag, an unassuming man with a quiet demeanour, possessed one of the sharpest brains in the republican movement. Even before the second round of negotiations with the Mountain Climber began, he was sending Bik and Adams frequent comms that questioned the wisdom of continuing with the hunger strike, on the basis of our negotiating strategy. In those comms, some of which I read at the time, he expressed the view that he felt that the hunger strikers who were still on the fast were dying for each other because they hadn't any chance of achieving the five demands. He continually asked what the 'bottom line' was: 'How can the Brits know what we want – *I* don't even know.'

To reinforce that point, Pat Beag confided to Bik that he was 'critical of the outside's handling of the Mountain Climber initiative, and feel that Adams and company should have been more flexible and met the Foreign Office negotiator halfway'.

Pat Beag's situation was bizarre. Here was a man who was prepared to die on hunger strike, and yet he didn't know what it would take to save his life. Bik could offer him no answers because he didn't know himself. All Bik could do in relation to Pat Beag's queries was to repeat the line that a flexible solution would manifest itself if the British wanted to settle. At no time during the hunger strike did Adams, on behalf of the external leadership, explain to us what would be a reasonable settlement in their eyes.

Therein lay one of the three fundamental weaknesses in our tactics. Besides the debilitating one-man-at-a-time tactic, we had never discussed what would be the minimum concessions we would accept to bring about an end to the hunger strike with integrity before the strike started. And not having discussed what would have been the minimum payload for us, we never sought the Army Council's view on what were its minimum requirements. Part and parcel to this lack of clarity was the limitations of the comm system. There were no face-to-face debates between the outside leadership and the prison leadership and therefore no broad discussions where conflicting views could be tested. Moreover, as IRA Volunteers, we were duty-bound to adhere to the Army Council's summation of the situation; even so, the possibility that the Council would disagree with a settlement that was acceptable to us had never entered our heads. Indeed, such was the limited scope of our deliberations that, until I hit on the idea of composing the 4 July statement, we had not even set about defining the exact nature of the five demands.

On 28 July, Bik wrote Adams a very important comm. Such is its significance that it needs to be reproduced in full:

To Brownie [Gerry Adams] Tuesday 28.7.81 from Bik 10.30 pm

Comrade Mór, just back from the hospital – fearful sight altogether. The boys sent for me and I had an

hour with them. Firstly, the Lynch family
[Barabbas's family], in conjunction with the
Menace [Father Faul], intend to release a public
statement tonight or tomorrow calling for an end to
the hunger strike. I saw Kevin but he couldn't talk,
see or hear me. He was lapsing into unconscious-
ness every few minutes. Very bad state altogether.
His brother was there, but I didn't get talking to
him. I just nodded to him. He was looking [for]
signs of hope from me I suppose. I saw Doc [Kieran
Doherty]. He's somewhat delirious, but was able to
tell me he's strong and determined and maintains
the line. Now I spent the best part of an hour with
the other lads discussing some points which arose
today. 1. Paddy Quinn had a visit with his brother
who told him that two SDLP boyos (McAvoy and
some other efforts) had contact with an NIO
[Northern Ireland Office] official who told them we
could get clothes, something on remission and
something on segregation, but that work remains
the same. A load of balls, as you can see. However,
Paddy said he couldn't speak for everyone, just
himself, and that personally he would be interested
to hear what the SDLP boys actually had. The
second pointer today arose when Tom [McElwee]
had a visit with Father Oliver Crilly, who put a
proposal to him – as the hunger strike stands now,
he said, both parties are almost at the peak of a
mountain, but neither wants to make the first move.
We should make that move, he says, thus moving
directly to that peak. From there we can enjoy
universal acclaim and support which would insist in
ensuring that a settlement is arrived at. Now the
whole business is along the Bishop Daly proposal

[Daly advocated calling an end to the hunger strike in order to allow public opinion, and influential individuals, to be given a further chance to move the British]. I tore it to shreds and pointed out that the moment the hunger strike stopped then cosmetic reforms would be the order of the day and *sin sin* ['that's that']. I told him straight that the decision was theirs − either we pursue course for the five demands or we capitulate. No in-between solutions. Tom then pointed out to me that he wasn't on about 'half a loaf', but just a possible change in tactics to secure the five demands. I said we should keep firmly to our line and not deviate in the slightest, because to do so spelt danger. They expressed concern about saving the lads' lives if a way could be found through a change of tactics. However, they accepted that the offers floating about were of little or no relevance at all. They all say they are strong mentally and determined to carry on. They say they realise it could mean their deaths, but they understand this. They expressed concern about the pressure swinging towards us, and the Brits using me as an excuse for not talking. (The papers haven't been too healthy since last week, as you know.) They were thinking of a way to turn the tables on the Brits and expose them as having nothing to offer. They proposed that I take a back seat and allow them to see NIO reps so that they can get rid of this red herring for good. I explained the position that my presence was essential at any negotiations and that a break in the line now would hammer us in the future. Also, that keeping firmly in line weighed far heavier in the balance than a propaganda exercise. I said that you lot were doing your utmost to ensure that bad propaganda was warded off and that you'd counteract Brit moves. The boys said you were making heavy weather of this last week. I explained how you were on the ball every day pulling Amadon II [Dr Garret FitzGerald, the Irish Taoiseach] back into the firing line and that we'd gone through periods of unfavourable press coverage before. I told them that we could always expect things to run like this, but that we'd managed to get above the situation alright. I said that you lot were in the best position to advise and to read the situation and that you'd agreed that my presence is a must at any talks. Also that you'd ensure a hundred percent effort and more to steering the propaganda in the right direction. Paddy expressed the opinion that once Doc and Kevin died, then we couldn't really expect further pressure to build on the Brits, even if they were all drawing close to death. He felt that there'll come a time when we'd have to make a move. I put our position straight to them all. Firstly, that cutting me out to gain a propaganda victory was dangerous and that it in itself would not save the boys' lives. Secondly, that we had two options – 1. pursue our course for the five demands, or 2. capitulate now. I told them I could have accepted half-measures before Joe McDonnell died, but I didn't then and wouldn't now. I said the Brits took a firm stand last week but had also acknowledged that somewhere along the line they may be forced to meet our demands. I then asked them for an opinion and they each told me that they'd continue and maintain the line. They are strong, *cara*. I think last week's propaganda had an effect on their

morale slightly . . . Tom mentioned about the possibility of me going on hunger strike so that no
matter what moves were afoot I'd be in the middle
of things and could ward off Brit propaganda
tactics. I just told him there was little chance of me
getting permission and it wouldn't help things
anyway. Once we get rid of one red herring, the
Brits would just fish another one to suit. I had to
explain to them all that I had been an advocate of
hunger strike from last year and should have been
on the first hunger strike, only you lot, or else Bob
[Sands] and Dark, recognised me as a disaster area.
I told them I wanted to be on this hunger strike, but
Bob wouldn't even listen to me. Tom knows the
score as he was in the wing with me from [when] we
came from H6 in '79. I told him I mentioned to Tish
[Jim Gibney, a member of the republican mon-
itoring committee] on a visit shortly after Bob died
that I wanted to go on hunger strike and he told me
I was crazy. Anyway, you all realise I would be a
propaganda liability. If it makes any difference, *cara*,
I don't believe I would be, not any more anyhow. I
no longer accept the argument that tore lumps out
of me last year. I have had more publicity lately than
Prince Charles and not a word about it. Prop-
aganda-wise (good or bad) I'm burnt out. I have
always wanted to be on that front line and I haven't
changed one iota. I should be there *sin é* and I still
want to be there. I've no need to tell you what
degree of commitment I have or how much
understanding of the situation I have. You know I'd
do my best and I know I'd die *sin é*. I'll abide by your
decision as I can do little else. If it's negative just say
no. Please don't forward any explanations. I just

wouldn't accept them and that's the truth, *cara*. I'd appreciate it also if you'd refrain from giving me a lecture!! I think I've covered everything. I've told the boys they shouldn't send for me unless it's urgent, as numerous visits don't really help much. It's not that I don't want to be up there. That's the truth, *cara*. Though I must be honest and tell you that tonight's episode wrecked me. But I'm sound enough now. Please don't think my request for [a] place on hunger strike has come [now]. I was boxing it off last week only Ricky [O'Rawe] cut me to shreds, and convinced me I'd be wasting my time.

Why is this comm so significant? First, it didn't reach Adams until the morning of the next day, 29 July. On the night that Bik wrote the comm from his cell in H3, Adams was convening an urgent meeting in Belfast at the request of Father Faul and the families of the hunger strikers. At that meeting, Adams hesitated when some of the families asked him to go into the prison and inform their loved ones that they should abandon their fast. Upon receipt of Bik's comm, though, Adams became aware of the possibility that the Lynch family was contemplating releasing a press statement calling for the hunger strike to be ended. Had that statement been released, it would have represented a body blow to the continuation of the strike. What impact this development had on Adams I don't know, but before lunch he phoned Father Faul to tell him that he would go into the prison after all. Father Faul informed Cardinal Ó Fiaich, and the Cardinal made the necessary arrangements with the NIO.

Second, it was obvious from the tone of Bik's comm that a meeting had taken place between the six conscious hunger strikers (Big Doc and Kevin Lynch being omitted because of their physical deterioration) before they sent for Bik to come to the camp hospital on the night of 28 July. Those in attendance were Tom McElwee, Micky Devine, Pat Beag McGeown, Matt Devlin, Paddy Quinn and Lorny McKeown. At the meeting, it seems that some, if not all, of these six were unhappy about our tactics. Paddy Quinn thought that we should at least hear what exactly the two SDLP men (who were in contact with his brother) had to offer.

There is an understandable logic in what Paddy was saying, and at face value there was nothing to be lost in giving them a hearing. The danger was, however – and Bik saw this – that once the SDLP had got their foot in the door we could have been into another commission scenario, and our previous experience with the commission had been disastrous. What they had been talking about then had raised false hopes and didn't even measure up to the Mountain Climber proposals. With the two-option line now the benchmark for future policy, coupled with the Army Council's rejection of the Mountain Climber deal and the Mountain Climber's declaration that no British government could concede the five demands, Bik was right in his assessment that there was no merit in raising false hopes by sussing out the SDLP initiative.

When Bik rejected Paddy's opinion, Tom McElwee came in and asked for a change of tactics. Specifically, Tom wanted Bik to drop out of the picture in order to give the British government room to negotiate directly with the hunger strikers, thus allowing them the comfort of saying they were not recognising the IRA command structure. In order to sweeten this departure from our negotiating position, Tom offered the possibility that, by allowing the hunger strikers to negotiate alone, they could remove the 'red herring' (that Bik's presence was an impediment to a settlement) for good and expose the British for having nothing to offer. Bik rejected this, saying that 'you lot were in the best position to advise and to read the situation and that you'd agreed that my presence is a must at any talks'. Faced with an impregnable wall, Tom changed tack and asked Bik to go on hunger strike to see what the British would offer. Bik blocked this route also, saying that there was 'little chance of me getting permission and it wouldn't help things anyway' – both of which were true.

Then Paddy Quinn came right out with it and told Bik that when Big Doc and Kevin Lynch died, we (the prisoners) couldn't expect any further pressure to build on the British, even if they (the hunger strikers) were all drawing close to death. He felt that there would come a time when we would have to make the first move.

Paddy was stating the obvious; but why then let Big Doc and Kevin die at all? How would their deaths alter the situation? The question is: was Paddy expressing a personal opinion or a collective one? Pat Beag's comms and criticisms of our tactics had left no room for doubt as to how he felt about continuing with the hunger strike. He also said that Micky Devine, an INLA hunger striker, had told him: 'Look, I think we need to call an end to this. Somebody has to take a decision to call an end to it.' So according to this, there were at least four of the hunger strikers who were unhappy with our tactics.

This conversation between Pat Beag and Micky took an interesting turn when Pat Beag agreed the following:

Since the doctors reckoned Micky had ten days or so left, and ten days would have taken us over the Owen Carron election [Carron was the Sinn Féin candidate in the by-election that would be held to replace Bobby Sands], I said to him 'Hold out for the ten days.' After the Fermanagh/South Tyrone by-election, I didn't see any political point in us continuing the hunger strike, and I'll be saying that quite openly.

Tragically, Pat Beag never had the opportunity to call for an end to the hunger strike because, as forecast by the prison doctors, Micky Devine died ten days later, on the day that Owen Carron was elected. Pat Beag went into the death coma on the same day.

Pat Beag's words to Micky bring us to what he has come, over time, to recognise as the crux of the hunger strike: the political kudos that the hunger strike would bring for the republican movement. He makes it clear that Micky, and for that matter he himself, should endanger his life to get Carron elected. The question arises: was this the agenda that the republican leadership had been working towards from the moment that Bobby Sands died? Was that why they had rejected the prison leadership's acceptance of the Mountain Climber's offer before Joe McDonnell died? Put another way: why hide the existence of the Mountain Climber from the families and hide our acceptance of the deal from the hunger strikers? One thing is certain: the hitherto-accepted line that the prison leadership and the hunger strikers were controlling events does not stand up to scrutiny.

Bik replied to Paddy by telling the hunger strikers that they had two options: pursue our course for the five demands, or capitulate immediately. 'I told them that I could have accepted half-measures before Joe [McDonnell] died but that I didn't then and wouldn't now.'

Those 'half-measures' were a reference to the first Mountain Climber's proposals. I have to say I was taken aback and vexed when I first read this comm in 1985. Clearly Bik is relating to Adams the conversation that he had had with the hunger strikers the previous night and, taken at face value, one would have to assume that Bik was being less than forthright with the hunger strikers because he *did* in fact accept the proposals. I spent a considerable amount of time thinking about this and concluded that Bik was being truthful to the hunger strikers. This is because, in light of the Army Council's rejection of the Mountain Climber's offer, both he and I had unambiguously accepted the view of our peers.

The thrust of Bik's lengthy comm to Adams conveys the message that the hunger strikers were effectively relegated to the role of Sherpas in the hunger strike: they could die carrying the equipment for the republican mountain climbers, but they had no influence on what route the climbers were taking to reach the summit.

Difficult as it may seem for an outsider to understand, Bik's role in all this was subject to the laws of command and control. His authority had been critically undermined by the Army Council's rejection of the Mountain Climber deal before Joe McDonnell died. After that, he was a mere extension of the Army Council, condemned to take orders or advice from them. In the absence of an order from the Council to end the hunger strike, he saw his role as following the Army Council line. If his voice had been listened to way back when the Mountain Climber had made his offer, Joe McDonnell and the five other prisoners who died after him would be alive today.

22

While Bik was writing his 28 July comm to Adams, outlining the reservations of some hunger strikers, Father Faul was also busy, gathering together the families of the eight remaining hunger strikers in a hotel in Toomebridge, County Antrim. At that meeting, he told them that he was convinced that Thatcher was not going to give in to the five demands and that they should have a meeting with Adams – the man at whose desk, as Bik had reportedly said in a conversation with Father Faul, 'the buck really stops'. At the subsequent meeting with the families in the Sinn Féin centre in Belfast that night, Adams explained this away by producing a comm from Bik which illustrated that the comment had been made in the context of Bobby insisting on Adams's presence if he had met with the European Commission for Human Rights.

So what exactly was Adams's role in the hunger strike? He was juggling numerous balls in the air, the principal one being co-ordinating the republican response to the hunger strike. He was the power behind the National H-Block/Armagh Committee. As well as that, he was striving dutifully to ensure that a rich political harvest would be reaped by the republican movement from the fast – a task he completed very successfully. His workload also included liaising between the Army Council and the prison leadership. (I used to enjoy reading Adams's comms. His inimitable scribbles were almost indecipherable, but after reading them a couple of times I always came away with the feeling that Adams was intellectually and politically light years ahead of the rest of us – which he was.) In addition, the leading authors on books about the hunger strike, David Beresford and Padraig O'Malley, accepted that Adams assumed personal charge of the negotiations with the Mountain Climber (Beresford said that 'Gerry Adams was in a safe house in west Belfast, waiting by the telephone for more messages from the Foreign Office contact, the Mountain Climber'). That put a huge burden on Adams – even if he did consult with a few others. He had the responsibility of passing judgment on what was, and what wasn't, an acceptable deal; his communications with the Mountain Climber could have spelt life or death for his comrades on hunger strike in the H-Blocks. Unfortunately for those trapped by the ghosts of comrades dead, he was never positive in his assessment of what was on offer.

For security reasons, the families of the hunger strikers, along with Father Faul, went from the Toomebridge meeting that night to the Sinn Féin headquarters in Belfast and met Gerry Adams and other leading republicans. The families asked Adams to go into Long Kesh and tell the hunger strikers how hopeless the situation was. (Most of the hunger strikers already knew this; even as Adams was meeting the families, Bik was sitting in his cell writing his comm to him confirming their feeling of hopelessness.)

Father Faul had a different agenda: he wanted Adams

to order an end to the strike. Adams told the families that the Army Council had been opposed to the hunger strike from the start and had agreed to the request only after much pleading from the prisoners. This is correct. Adams also told the families: 'The IRA could not order an end to the hunger strike.' But he then went on to say, when asked if he would request the Army Council to call it off, that, 'It would take days for its members to get together and consider it.'

One statement contradicts the other. Of course the IRA could always have called off the hunger strike – as anyone with even a minute knowledge of the IRA knows – and they eventually did. Adams agreed to pass on the families' request to the Army Council (although what happened at that Army Council meeting, if it ever took place, was never disclosed). It appears that the meeting between the republican leaders and the families broke up without the issue being resolved.

Sometimes it's the dog that doesn't bark that tells the biggest tale. At that gathering, neither Adams nor any of the leading republicans informed the families that the British government had already been in contact with the IRA leadership and had offered substantial concessions which the prison leadership had accepted. Why weren't they told? The answer, as before, is that a 'need-to-know' pyramid was in place.

At the top of that pyramid was Adams, the communicator with the prisoners, the public face of the republican movement and the silent negotiator. He had at least one confidant who was privy to the negotiations with the Mountain Climber. As I found out years later, other members of the committee that had been set up by the Army Council to monitor the hunger strike were not informed about the more sensitive negotiations.

I do not know the extent to which the Army Council were briefed. I would assume that they were given a detailed account of the hunger strike, although, because they did not have first-hand experience of the situation, it is difficult to see how they could have fully understood the complexities and political permutations of the fast.

Next came Bik. He would have been aware of all aspects relating directly to the maintenance of the hunger strike, but if there had been an agenda that differed from bringing the fast to a successful conclusion, he would not have been aware of it. That information would have been the preserve of a handful of people.

Then there was myself, and possibly Jake Jackson. We had been more than willing to accept the Mountain Climber deal, but I'm not sure that Bik had informed Jake of our decision (although he knew of the initiative).

As well as us, the eight hunger strikers knew about the Mountain Climber proposals, but, in my view, they had been conditioned by the IRA leadership into believing that those proposals constituted an unacceptable compromise. Recently I had occasion to speak to one of the surviving hunger strikers. During the course of our conversation I asked him if he was aware that Bik and I had accepted the first Mountain Climber proposals and had sent a communication to that effect to the outside leadership. He was obviously taken aback by this knowledge, so much so, that he remarked 'That's news to me.' This corresponds with my understanding of the situation, which is that Bik and I were the only prisoners who were aware that we had approved the proposals. I had no idea how much information was being given to the hunger strikers. I am, though, fairly certain that no one informed them that we had accepted the deal. My inexcusable failure to recognise, at the time, the importance of the hunger strikers being aware of all aspects pertaining to their fast, is one of the main reasons for me now breaking my silence. There has been no mention in any of the hunger strike books of the prison leadership accepting the proposals. This suggests that someone had taken a decision to keep this information from the hunger strikers. I don't know who made that decision. Nor am I going to speculate on why they would do so.

Next on the pyramid of awareness were Seanna Walsh and the three Block OCs. I believe that Seanna knew of the Mountain Climber initiative, but I am certain he didn't know that we were willing to accept the deal. (He told me as much when, in 2003, I bumped into him in west Belfast and asked him if he knew that we had accepted the deal before Joe McDonnell died. His reply was that he didn't.) The Blocks' OCs were given very limited information, usually hints that things were happening behind the scenes.

Last, there were the ordinary Blanketmen, the hunger strikers' families and finally the general public. None of these groups knew anything of the Mountain Climber or deals of any kind. One logical explanation for the hunger strikers' families knowing nothing is that the Army Council perceived the families as the weak link in the chain: the families had the potential to end the hunger strike – which was becoming, increasingly, the worst of all options for those who controlled the strike. The main concern of the families, naturally, was to save the lives of their loved ones, rather than to secure the five demands. Had they known the details of the Mountain Climber's offer, they would very likely have accepted it, or at least openly criticised either the prison leadership or the Army Council for rejecting the proposals. Finally, the hunger strikers may themselves have decided not to tell their families about what was happening.

The next day, 29 July, possibly after receiving Bik's lengthy comm Adams agreed to come into Long Kesh. Father Faul had to content himself with Adams's promise that he would give the hunger strikers a full and frank analysis of the fact that the five demands might never be delivered – which, in fairness, Adams did.

That night, Adams, Owen Carron (the prospective H-Block candidate for Bobby Sands's Westminster seat) and INLA representative Seamus Ruddy were allowed into the camp hospital to see Bik and the hunger strikers. Big Doc and Kevin Lynch were too ill to join the others in the hospital canteen. The six hunger strikers who met the three men were Paddy Quinn, Tom McElwee, 'Red Mick' Devine, Matt Devlin, Pat Beag and Lorny McKeown. Bik was also present.

According to David Beresford, writing in *Ten Men Dead*, Adams told the men what the Mountain Climber had offered:

Prison uniforms would be abolished; they would get their own clothes. Their demands would be met on visits, letters and parcels. There would be effective, although unofficial, segregation. Work would be ambiguously defined, to include educational courses and handicrafts. There would be free association throughout weekends and for three hours every weekday. And the government would phrase the deal in conciliatory terms.

The proposals that Adams outlined to the hunger strikers were the substance of what the Mountain

Climber had been offering before Joe McDonnell's death.

The facts, though, are different from how they appear at first glance. Adams wasn't giving the hunger strikers the option of accepting or rejecting the proposals: he had already rejected them on their behalf, and the Mountain Climber had long since begun his descent from the peak of what was achievable. Why then present the hunger strikers with the proposals at all? One answer is that the Big Lad may have suspected that, at some stage in the future, someone would clinically examine his role in the hunger strike, and he wanted to put some distance between the crucial decisions and himself and feed the illusion that the hunger strikers had had a voice in the decision-making process; he used David Beresford to create that illusion in *Ten Men Dead*. When closely examined, *Ten Men Dead* lacks detail and deals in generalities. (To be fair to Beresford, he was not to know the extent to which he was being used. He had to deal with the facts as he was told them by the republican leadership of the time.) Another answer is that Adams knew, even before he went into the prison hospital, that the hunger strikers would unquestionably accept the leadership's decision to reject the Mountain Climber's proposals. To make sure that an inappropriate reception didn't await him, Pat Beag McGeown, the only man who would not have been intimidated by Adams's reputation and stature within the republican movement, had been told to keep his mouth shut.

That said, Adams never spared the rod in telling the strikers how bleak the situation was or how unlikely the prospects of further concessions were. He told them: 'You eight could be dead and another five or six could be dead and you might still not get your five demands.' He also went in to see Kevin Lynch and Big Doc in their rooms and told Big Doc: 'I can go out now, Doc, and announce it's over.' No one can accuse Adams of softening the harsh reality of the strikers' predicament and of not offering them the opportunity to end it themselves. Nor can he be indicted for not telling them that the republican movement would back any decision they made and that there would be no damage done if they ended their fast.

On the other hand, he never told them that their prison leadership had accepted the Mountain Climber's proposals before Joe McDonnell had died and that the Army Council had rejected that acceptance.

Perhaps Adams hoped that the bleak picture he was painting would be enough to persuade the eight men to end their hunger strike. If so, he was mistaken. Those with only a cursory knowledge of the situation could see that the prison leadership and the hunger strikers would always defer to the authority of the Army Council, even if they thought the situation was beyond recovery. As Pat Beag put it, the hunger strikers 'would be the last ones to make a decision to come off it', because of the one-man-at-a-time strategy.

If the Army Council really wanted the hunger strikers to end their protest, there was another route that could have been taken. The Council could have asked Adams to present their formal opinion to the strikers that the fast had run its course and should be terminated, while leaving the final decision up to the hunger strikers. Such an approach would, I believe, have been enough to bring about the cessation of the hunger strike and would also have maintained the illusion that the prisoners and the hunger strikers were, and had always been, in total control of the hunger strike. It would also have got the

Army Council off the hook for making what were, in my opinion, some fatally flawed decisions.

According to Pat Beag, before the meeting he had been told: 'Don't make your opinions known.' Someone didn't want Adams to be given a rough ride. The only possible reason for gagging Pat Beag is that at least half, if not more, of the surviving hunger strikers had accepted his analysis of the situation (that the situation was irretrievable), and whoever was ultimately responsible for his silencing believed that he had the potential to generate a debate that might well have forced an end to the strike – which they obviously didn't want.

It should be borne in mind that, along with Pat Beag, Paddy Quinn, Red Mick Devine and possibly Tom McElwee were also questioning the logic of continuing the hunger strike. (Bik had informed Adams and the Army Council of this in his comm of the previous day, 28 July.) It appears that Adams did not refer to their expressed reservations at the meeting. Why not? If he, on behalf of the Army Council, really wanted the hunger strike to end, this was the golden opportunity to persuade the strikers to stop their fast. If the movement really wanted it stopped, why not urge Pat Beag to speak out and influence the others to end the strike? Conversely, in the face of Pat Beag's uncharacteristic silence, why didn't Gerry ask him what his opinion was?

The revelation that Pat Beag had been silenced came to my attention only years later, when I read of an interview he had given to Padraig O'Malley for O'Malley's book *Biting at the Grave*. I cringed when I read that he had been gagged. No man facing death by hunger strike deserves to be treated so disgracefully.

I believe the stifling of Pat Beag's opinion and Gerry

Adams's silence in the face of Bik's 28 July comm ensured that more men would die. The lamentable paradox of the situation struck me when, after Adams had left, Pat Beag stated that: 'I came under considerable pressure from the lads [hunger strikers] in the hospital.' The hunger strikers were asking him if the situation was as bad as Adams had portrayed it, to which he replied: 'My answer should have been yes, but what I have to do is to say: "Well there's an angle here, there's an angle there, we might be able to work something out."'

It was a tragedy of tragedies. It seemed as if the next man to die did not want to be seen to pull the plug on the hunger strike. His courage overrode all other considerations. Even though the hunger strikers knew that the chance of winning all five demands was remote in the extreme, they were still prepared to give their lives, rather than be seen to ask Adams to call off the hunger strike, in case they were perceived to be letting down both their dead comrades and themselves.

The episode was pitiful; a golden opportunity had been lost. Pat Beag died in October 1996. Some say his death was attributed to ill health caused by the time he had spent on hunger strike. He has often been referred to as 'the eleventh hunger striker'.

23

At the end of July, Paddy Quinn went into a coma and his mother intervened to save his life. It was a courageous decision, and Paddy eventually recovered. The stress the families must have been under cannot be imagined. To sit day after day and watch your husband or son, a fine healthy young man in the prime of his life, lose his sight and hearing, and then have his vital organs collapse, must be an unearthly ordeal. I couldn't blame any mother for taking her son off hunger strike when he had gone into a coma. Whether they decided to abide by their loved ones' wishes and let them die, or intervened to save them, the families were every bit as heroic as the hunger strikers.

On 1 August, Kevin Lynch died. He had been seventy-one days on hunger strike and was twenty-five years old. Kevin was known as 'Barabbas', but we also affectionately nicknamed him 'The Gem of the Roe' because he lived in Dungiven, County Derry, beside the River Roe. He was a great guy. His INLA comrade and friend from Dungiven, Liam McCloskey, replaced him on hunger strike.

Kieran Doherty (Big Doc) died the next day, after seventy-three days on hunger strike. Kieran was twenty-five years old and the TD for Cavan/Monaghan.

Pat Sheehan from Belfast replaced him. Nothing I can say would do these two men justice, but there was a hole in my heart after their deaths. I was beside myself with grief.

Tom McElwee died on 8 August. He was the ninth hunger striker to die and was only twenty-three years old. Jackie McMullan from Belfast replaced him on hunger strike.

On hearing of Tom's death, Bik commed Gerry Adams, describing Big Tom as 'a terrific character – a pillar of strength here, with the deep respect of every last Blanketman'. Those words very accurately summed up Tom McElwee's spirit: he faced hard situations head-on. The screws were afraid of him because it mattered little to him whether two or twenty-two of them were surrounding him, or whether he was naked or not: if they tried to beat him up, they knew he would go down fighting. Bullies and cowards hate the Tom McElwees of this world.

In that comm, Bik went on to tell Adams that:

> The IRSP [the political wing of the INLA] have no further replacements so I intend to use our men, unless you feel we shouldn't for some reason or other.

Bik is clearly defining the command structure here. He is not saying that we shouldn't replace Tom – far from it – but he is acknowledging the final authority of the Army Council in the decision about whether or not a replacement should go on hunger strike. He is intimating that, if the Army Council decides not to replace Tom, whether because the IRSP has no replacements or, crucially, because the Council wishes to end the hunger strike, then that is the Council's prerogative. If the Army Council had replied that Tom McElwee should not be replaced, then that would have effectively spelled the end of the hunger strike. No comm came in telling Bik not to replace Tom.

I decided that I should at least try to get the Mountain Climber to contact us again, so on 6 August I drew up a statement which, in tone, was even more conciliatory than that of 4 July. I also pleaded with the SDLP, the Catholic Church and the Irish government to support our five demands in order to keep the pressure on the British. Again, I specifically asked the SDLP to withdraw its local councillors from the Council Chambers. The party did not even acknowledge the statement. The British government said that there was nothing new in it.

On 20 August, Red Mick Devine became the tenth hunger striker to die. He was a member of the INLA, twenty-seven years old and married with two children. This poor man – like his nine comrades – was blessed (or damned) with the heart of a lion. He had told Pat Beag that he thought all was lost, yet he chose to forfeit his life rather than end his hunger strike. What naked valour! He had one life, and he gave it for us. On the same day, Pat Beag's wife, Pauline, intervened to save his life when he went into a coma.

The number of men who had died on hunger strike had reached double figures. I couldn't comprehend how things had come to this. We had never envisaged Joe McDonnell dead, never mind another five comrades as well. I asked myself: 'Where the hell did we go wrong?' Meanwhile, the hunger strike was in serious difficulties because the relatives of Matt Devlin and Lorny

McKeown took their example from the Quinn and McGeown families and intervened to save the lives of their kinfolk when they went into a coma.

Bernard Fox ended his hunger strike on 25 September because of excruciating stomach complaints. The next day, Liam McCloskey from Dungiven came off hunger strike after fifty-five days. Word reached us that Gerry Carville, a hunger striker from County Down, had also decided to withdraw.

I came to the conclusion that there was no way back for us and that all hope was gone. There was no chance of us getting our five demands, and people were dying for each other rather than for the demands. I had known this for a long time but had ignored it, and along with that I had ignored my responsibilities as a leader in the forsaken hope that I was wrong. Our tears had made us blind to a grim reality, but there were no more tears left to shed. I could no longer keep quiet. For the sake of my sanity, I decided I had to break with the party line and speak out.

During a talk with The Dark at Mass on 29 September, I found an ally – someone who had reached the same conclusions as I had. I agreed to comm Bik and present our joint view that all was lost. Back in my cell, I wrote to Bik to tell him that both The Dark and I believed that we should call off the hunger strike immediately.

Bik wrote back accepting that we had difficulties, but he said that we could overcome the problem of family intervention by moving men with more resolute families into the front line – men whose families had indicated to them that, come what may, they would abide by their sons' wishes. He felt that we could take the 'high ground' again, and that there was a list of men as long as your arm ready to go on hunger strike.

That night, though, Bik sent a comm to Adams:

Comrade Mór. 'Keep smiling at troubles, cause troubles are bubbles and bubbles will soon blow away.' I'm told that the author of that little piece is none other than 'Fat' Campbell, escapee extra-ordinaire, current resident in Portlaoise ....There is a growing feeling amongst those with what I would call a bit of savvy [The Dark and the author] that our present troubles may prove insurmountable. I have been asked to consider terminating the hunger strike. Now, that I will only consider when I believe we have no chance of regaining the top position and pushing forward towards a feasible solution. I don't believe that we should allow the action of a few clanns [families that took or were threatening to take their kin off the hunger strike] to dictate such action by us. We do face a critical few weeks, but I believe that we can overcome the problem.

What chance had we of 'regaining the top position'? None. What was 'a feasible solution'? The full five demands. Bik went on to tell Adams that, should the problem of families intervening to take their husbands and sons off hunger strike become 'insurmountable', then 'the reality of the situation would dictate an entire reappraisal'.

I sat on my bed and stared at the wall. I couldn't understand how Bik could still entertain the notion that we could take the 'top position' again. It just didn't make sense and was completely at odds with the stark reality of the situation.

Five families had already intervened to take their men off hunger strike, and more would certainly follow. The

British were not going to budge. Why should they? The interventions were leading to the collapse of the hunger strike. Moreover, the British had weathered the worst of it and did not need to do anything; no amount of fresh pressure could be worse than what they had already experienced.

As for having a list of volunteers as long as your arm to join the strike, I reckoned that there are times when bravery and big hearts are not enough. This was one of those times. The only thing left for us to do was to end the hunger strike.

The next day, a comm came in from the Army Council which echoed what I had said the previous day. Our problems were indeed insuperable, the comm said, and the Army Council ordered the strike to end. The comm stated that it should end six days later, on Saturday, 3 October 1981, at 3 PM. The leadership deliberately chose that time because the Sunday papers would have already gone to press and there would be a two-day gap to temper the expected triumphalism of the British gutter press.

Bik immediately abandoned his 'top position' assessment and did yet another *volte-face*, again accepting the Army Council's assessment. Why hadn't this order been given before Joe McDonnell died on 8 July, or when Gerry Adams visited the jail on 29 July?

On the day the hunger strike ended, six hunger strikers were still on the fast: Pat Sheehan, Jackie McMullan, Gerry Carville, John Pickering, Gerard Hodgins and Jim Devine. I had to prepare a closing statement. I was drained and emotionally exhausted by the enormity of all we had been through. The only consoling thought that night as I went to sleep was that no one else was going to die.

I began writing the final statement with fire in my belly. Here was an opportunity to castigate all those who had failed us and who, for their own narrow, selfish reasons, had refused to back our five demands. I wanted to make them hang their heads in shame and choke over their brandies and cigars when they read my words. I wanted them to know that, while they had sat in their easy chairs, ten valiant Irishmen had given their lives for their country, for their beliefs and for their comrades.

After giving a chronology of the events that had occurred during the hunger strike, I keelhauled the Catholic Church, the SDLP and the Dublin government for letting down our fallen comrades. I finished by saying:

> Our comrades have lit with their very lives an eternal beacon that will inspire this nation and people to rise and crush oppression forever, and this nation can be proud that it produced such a quality of manhood.
>
> We pay a special tribute to the families of our dead comrades. You have suffered greatly and with immense dignity. Your loved ones, our comrades and friends, were and would be proud of you for standing by them. No tribute is too great.
>
> Also, we give a special mention to those families who could not watch their loved ones die in pain and agony. We prisoners understand the pressure you were under and stand by you.
>
> We thank the National H-Block/Armagh movement, the nationalist people of Ireland and all those who championed our cause abroad. We are indebted to you and ask you to continue the good work on our behalf.

Lastly, we reaffirm our commitment to the achievement of the five demands by whatever means necessary and expedient. We rule nothing out. Under no circumstances are we going to devalue the memory of our dead comrades by submitting ourselves to a dehumanising and degrading regime.

For some inexplicable reason, God had forsaken us. He and I fell out for a long time after that. Ten of the Spartans were dead, but in death they had smashed the British government's resolve to pursue their criminalisation policy. British ministers tacitly admitted this by introducing a set of measures immediately after the hunger strike ended which included granting every prisoner in the North the right to wear his or her own clothes at all times. Running parallel with this, the British rarely again used any of the 'Godfather' jargon that had accompanied the introduction of the policy.

In the political sphere, the hunger strikers' sacrifice served to inform tens of thousands of people on the island of Ireland and in the outside world about the true nature of British involvement in our country, and that education provided the stimulus that would make us a confident people, a people committed to the principles that the hunger strikers had died for. (Many of the H-Block committees throughout the country became Sinn Féin *cumainn* overnight.) Sinn Féin, the political wing of the republican movement, would eventually grow to replace the SDLP, which steadfastly refused to support the five demands, as the voice of the majority of nationalists in the North.

Every hunger striker had earned the title 'hero'. They gave everything to the cause; they were superb.

24

Within a couple of days of the hunger strike ending, all prisoners in jails in the North were given their own clothes. Once we had our own clothes, we immediately claimed the right to one hour's exercise per day.

Men who had been buried in the H-Blocks for four years – some of whom hadn't taken even one visit and so hadn't walked under the sky during all the years of protest – were able to stretch their legs and greedily inhale clean, uncontaminated air. Even a sudden burst of rain was a joy as men turned their faces skyward to embrace the refreshing shower. The sheer pleasure of walking in company and chatting about different things was brilliant.

Very few of us spoke about the hunger strike, though. It seemed that, for a while at least, people wanted to expunge the stench of death; somehow to erase, even temporarily, the fact that ten comrades weren't with us any more, but were lying in cold graves. People needed time to adjust to the enormity of what had taken place, each in their own way.

I, for one, was gravely dejected. I was finding it difficult to come to terms with the role I had played in the hunger strike: the selection of hunger strikers, the issuing of statements and my silent acquiescence in the strategy discussions. I was overwhelmed by the enormity of the event in which I had so actively participated. I was also feeling guilty because I felt I could have done more to end the impasse. I should have been more outspoken in advocating acceptance of the Mountain Climber's proposals; I should have spoken up earlier than I did to call for an end to the strike.

The overriding problem of how we would progress persisted. Basically, we had two choices: either we went into the prison system with our own clothes, which was the option we had discussed before the hunger strike, and reconstruct the system along lines that were more to our liking, or we stayed put and served out our full time on protest.

Our opinion, to quote Bik in a comm sent to Adams on 3 October 1981, the day after the hunger strike ended, was that:

> We believe that we cannot hope to maintain a protest for a protracted period and therefore we must move ASAP to get ourselves above the present level – i.e. dispensing with blanket protest and trying to build up.

He went on to say: 'You can let me have an attitude to what way you lot view the situation.' By 'build up', Bik was talking about us abandoning any semblance of the blanket protest and moving *en masse* into the mainstream prison system with the intention of making it unworkable through disruption and sabotage. The option of continuing with the blanket protest wasn't really a runner: the prison struggle was over, the prisoners had given their all and to stay on a dormant protest would have been folly in the extreme.

The Army Council sent back a comm stating that under no circumstances should we consider accepting the prison regime. The Council believed that to do so would have been to besmirch the memory of our comrades who had died on the hunger strike. The thinking of the Council reflected the views of those on the outside who had no idea of the horrors that we had suffered during those four years and was removed from reality. It was tantamount to telling us to serve out our full sentences while accepting any privations that the prison authorities should deem to heap on us.

Volte-face number three followed. Bik again accepted the Council's view, even though he knew it was an absurd decision that was out of touch with reality. Rather than challenge the Army Council's thinking, or plead with its members to rethink their position, he again chose to follow the official line. Command structures; always command structures.

Not for me this time, however. That comm was the final straw. I remembered the agonising years of filthy protest and multiplied those by the deaths of my comrades. I decided to depart the protesting blocks forthwith. I wanted to leave all the doublespeak and posturing behind me. Whoever wanted the mantle of leadership could have it. I left H3 almost immediately after that Army Council comm was received and unquestionably accepted by Bik.

I was transferred to a conforming block, H1. Waiting there was a large contingent of fellow republicans, many of whom had spent up to four years on protest and who had left the protest in the days before the Army Council order.

But I was shocked to discover that there was no command structure in place in H1. My inbuilt sense of republicanism told me that no circumstances should exist in which IRA Volunteers 'did their own thing'. I could be criticised for seeking the security of a command structure after all that had happened during the hunger strike, but while I had had my fill of leadership, I was still an IRA Volunteer – and a committed republican. Yet even though the other republicans felt the same way, nobody wanted to take on the role or responsibility of leadership in H1. But someone had to take the job as Block OC and establish a structure there. Since it was clear that we would soon be confronting the loyalists on the segregation issue, it was important to get a structure in place as soon as possible. Following an order from Cleaky Clarke, who had been the OC of the conforming blocks, I very reluctantly took on the role, although I stipulated that it would be for a limited period only, or until we had sorted out the segregation issue.

The loyalists in H1 were a collection of oddballs and junkies. The number who queued up every morning and night to obtain mind-numbing drugs to help them do their time was compelling evidence that they were a motley crew. There were a few exceptions to the rule, but the majority didn't appear to be committed to anything except blanking out the pain of their incarceration.

Within a couple of weeks, the Army Council had to abandon the policy of perpetual protest because the conforming blocks started to fill up with former protesters. An order came down from our prison leadership that the loyalists were to be permanently locked up. By this time I had a good relationship with one of the prison officers, a decent and humane man who unofficially recognised our command structure. I asked to see him; during our meeting, I requested a meeting with Frankie Curry of the Ulster Volunteer Force to tell him that we wanted them to 'lock up' (refuse to leave their cells) at five o'clock that day. (Curry was on the other side of the block.) The prison officer's face turned white, and he asked me if there was no other way out for us. I repeated my view. Then he asked me what would happen if he refused to allow me see Curry. I shrugged; I told him that it didn't really matter if I saw Curry or not, that the only purpose of the meeting was to save the loyalists from serious injury – and possibly worse. He agreed to let me see Curry.

I found Curry to be a very polite and affable character. He told me how much he admired IRA Volunteers for their discipline and commitment to each other. While I appreciate compliments, I detest bullshit: his was the talk of a man who knew that he was skating on thin ice. (I couldn't forget his fearsome reputation for killing innocent Catholics. It was reported that, by the time he was eventually shot dead in a loyalist feud in March 1999, he had killed up to thirty Catholics.) When I gave Curry the ultimatum, he told me that there would be no problems from the UVF. I had already told the Ulster Defence Association CO about the five o'clock lock-up and had got the same reply.

At five o'clock, the loyalists wrecked their cells and spilled their piss under their cell doors. It was strange to be in a position where someone other than us was doing the wrecking. The screws did a cell count immediately afterwards. Within half an hour, the loyalists were moved off our wings, never to return.

Segregation was won throughout the H-Blocks – in

our case, without violence. Once it had been secured, I stood down as OC.

I later read an account from a loyalist leader, 'Twister' McQuistin of the UDA, in *Broadening the Battlefield* by Liam Clarke. His description of the republican prisoners made it clear why it was so easy for us to lock them up:

> If you argued with one of them, you argued with fifty. These guys were dedicated. They had done the blanket protests, dirty protests, and they had done the hunger strikes. They seemed to have an attitude that they were some sort of elite regiment, and when they came down they started getting into the loyalists. The loyalists went on protest to get away from them.

Once we had won segregation, we also secured control of the wings. Within two years, thirty-eight comrades, many of them former Blanketmen, including Bik, made a brilliant escape from the H-Blocks by hijacking the prison grub wagon. A screw was shot dead during the escape and nineteen comrades barged their way to freedom. The other nineteen were caught within the prison grounds. Three were later to die in SAS ambushes.

A report into that escape by Her Majesty's Inspector of Prisons paid my comrades a handsome compliment:

> They were quite unlike the population of any prison in England or Wales in their dangerousness, their allegiance to a paramilitary organisation, their cohesiveness, their common determination to escape and their resistance to the efforts of the prison authorities to treat them as ordinary criminals.

From that point on, the British deemed republican prisoners too dangerous to be allowed do prison work or move about the jail. This, along with a war of attrition in the wings, won them incremental gains right up until the British decided to grant them a conditional amnesty in 1998. The prisoners walked away from jail having won every demand that they had fought and died to achieve – and much more.

I was released in February 1983. On the night before my release, and with the wing in silence, I lay on top of my bed and thought of sweet and happy memories. There was Dollhead with his wee goatee beard calling Teapot up to the window to torture poor Hector about his 'missing the boat' with the women; Scull reading Seamus Heaney's poetry to Aidan Slane; The Dark with his melancholy eyes; and Bik singing 'All Right Now,' with Bobby on the bass. And Bobby, the irrepressible Bobby, the flaming soul of the protest, the spirit that would be forever free.

I must have been dreaming, for suddenly I'm walking along the seashore and a fresh yellow moon is rising above the waves. There are lights on the far shore, and I can make out the shape of a mountain, but I don't know where I am. Behind me is the dark-blue silhouette of an old castle, probably the scene of great and important battles in times gone by. A sharp blast of wind bites at my face.

I think I can see, out at sea, the shape of a large white cloud. It seems to be brilliant white, but maybe that's just a trick of light. The cloud appears to be moving very fast towards the shore and is billowing in on itself, creating a vortex effect. It's drawing nearer, nearer ....

The cloud opens up. Ten gigantic horsemen emerge and ride at full gallop directly towards me. The horses' white hooves make a splashing sound as they glide along the waves, and yet there's no spray. As they get closer, I notice that the horsemen have skeletal faces and long, white, monk-like hoods and habits.

They are almost on top of me. I know who they are; they are coming to take me away with them. They stop right in front of me and slowly turn their hooded heads in my direction. The lead horseman approaches me and, leaning down into my face, says, in that familiar husky voice: 'Risteard.' Bobby's bony hand strokes my face and I feel the warmth of the contact, the affection in the caress.

Then the horsemen turn and ride back into the cloud again, like spirits from another world. The sea swells up suddenly and I can hear singing, soft at first, then like thunder: 'Provos march on . . . .'

The lights go on in the cell; the ten horsemen are gone.

I am proud that I knew Bobby Sands and could call him and his fellow hunger strikers my good friends and comrades. Every time I think of Bobby's words to Father Faul – 'Greater love hath no man than to lay down his life for his friends' – it leaves me feeling desolate. Yet despite all the heartache, I am enormously grateful that God gave me the opportunity to have known those men.

Years later, I read Bobby's last comm to the outside world, a final testimony that summed up the spirit of the condemned man and those like him who gave all for our struggle:

> They won't break me, because the desire for freedom, and the freedom of the Irish people, is in my heart. The day will come when all the people of Ireland will have freedom in their hearts to show. It is then we'll see the Rising of the Moon.

'The Rising of the Moon' is the title of a rebel song summoning republicans to arms during the United

Irishmen's doomed rebellion of 1798. Five years later, Robert Emmet led another insurrection; he was condemned to be hanged, drawn and quartered when this rebellion too failed. In his dramatic speech from the dock, he said:

> Let no man write my epitaph . . . . When my country takes her place among the nations of the earth, then, and not until then, let my epitaph be written.

On that day, so shall the epitaph of my comrades be written.

EPILOGUE

While working with recovering alcoholics and drug addicts recently, I read a poem that had been written by one of them. This sixty-four-year-old man had lived in the back alleys and on the park benches of Belfast, London, Dublin and Dundalk. Describing his life's experiences in a poem, he wrote that: 'I died a thousand times to live.' During the three years it took me to complete this book, I got an understanding of what he was trying to say. The deeper I submerged myself in the hunger-strike story, the more I returned, emotionally, to that hideous little cell in H3 in the spring and summer of 1981.

In times of inner chaos, I would convince myself that I should walk away from the book, that I had a wonderful family and a secure future. My misgivings about proceeding with this book came from the fact that the noblest people I have met in my life are still members of the republican movement. Why should I stick my neck out and run the risk of being ostracised and maligned by my fellow republicans?

The crux of my concern was that, as I immersed myself in the fine detail of the story, I realised that, to avoid creating a whitewashed narrative, I would have no option but to question the actions of those comrades who had been involved at leadership level during the second hunger strike. That fact didn't sit comfortably with me. These were men whom I had known for decades and had counted among my friends. Yet, no matter how I struggled with this problem, I couldn't avoid the conclusion that my reluctance to stick my neck out had been part of the problem in the first place. Had I had the courage of my convictions during the second hunger strike and called for it to end sooner than I did, I could have lived comfortably in the knowledge that I had been true to myself and my dead comrades.

I am always hesitant about using general quotes when writing, primarily because one can trawl out a line or two to suit any situation. But I came across something that Voltaire, the eighteenth-century French writer and philosopher, believed and that went to the heart of what I am trying to say: 'We owe respect to the living; to the dead we owe only truth.' In the end, I too arrived, in good conscience, at a simple conclusion: I owed a debt to those ten heroic men who so bravely led the way and who were so electrified by the righteousness of our cause that they willingly sacrificed their lives.

I want to make clear that this book is not the definitive story of the second hunger strike. This is principally because I was not privy to the IRA leadership's thinking in relation to the Mountain Climber's proposals.

In order to get a broader understanding of this narrative, it is important to revisit some of the more pertinent aspects of the hunger strike. One thing sticks out above all others: Maggie Thatcher, the British prime minister, and the British state ignored opportunities to end the dispute honourably during the Cardinal Ó Fiaich/NIO talks. (The now deceased Cardinal deserves special praise for his attempts to bring an end to the impasse and to avoid the hunger strikes; his humanity shone out like the Star of Bethlehem.) The British government did so because they believed that, by standing firm, they could defeat the prisoners and deal a mortal blow to the armed struggle. In seeking outright victory, they left us with no choice but to embark on the hunger strike. Therefore, they are ultimately responsible for the deaths of the ten hunger strikers in the H-Blocks in 1981.

Another salient point is that the IRA Army Council strenuously opposed both hunger strikes. The Army Council acceded to our requests for permission to go on both hunger strikes only after we had put them under huge moral pressure.

The prison leadership accepted the first Mountain Climber deal days before Joe McDonnell died. The Army Council overruled us, ostensibly on the grounds that there would probably be a second, improved offer. The prisoners' leadership accepted this analysis without reservation. With Joe's premature death, the second offer never materialised; after his death, we were catapulted into a protracted hunger strike.

The Army Council did not advocate the ending of the hunger strike until weeks after the tenth man had died, when it was apparent that the families would intervene *en masse* to bring their loved ones off the fast.

The heartbreak engendered by the second hunger strike wasn't just confined to the H-Blocks, but affected the general public as well. Twenty-five people died in the North between 5 May and 3 October 1980. In the same period of 1981 (from Bobby Sands's death to the day the hunger strike ended), sixty-five people lost their lives. As usual, the civilian population, of whom twenty-five people were killed, paid the highest price. The security forces lost twenty-four members, while there were sixteen republican casualties (including the ten hunger strikers). During the hunger strike, inter-communal strife was rampant as both sections of society in the North of Ireland retreated into their traditional enclaves. It would take another seventeen years after the end of the second hunger strike before the two sections of our people trusted each other enough to reach an accommodation, which manifested itself in the Good Friday Agreement. (And even then there were elements on both sides that opposed the accord.)

At the time of writing, some fifty former Blanketmen have died since 1981. Some were killed on active service; others were assassinated by loyalists; most, including Kieran Nugent, the first Blanketman, died of natural causes.

While those are the bare facts, it is important to look at the broader consequences of the second hunger strike, because without doubt it was the key moment of departure from the armed-struggle strategy. It split the atom in terms of republican policy; the confidence generated by the enormous groundswell of political support that arose from the tragedy convinced influential people, not least Gerry Adams, that there were strategic options open to us other than perpetual war. A seed had taken root that would grow into the peace process. No matter how history chooses to judge Adams in relation to the second hunger strike – and I have been critical of him in this book – one thing is certain: without him and the hunger strikers, there would be no semblance of peace in Ireland today. Adams, more than anyone, saw the debilitating limitations of the armed-struggle approach and steered the republican movement away from potential obscurity and irrelevance to the position of political strength that it enjoys in the nationalist community in the North of Ireland today. He, and the inner circle of political activists who surround him, has also transformed Sinn Féin in the South of Ireland from an unelectable, irrelevant party to a force in Dáil Éireann. While we Blanketmen in H3 looked despairingly at our political Everest and K2 during our debate on the future direction of the struggle back in the unforgiving winter of 1980/81, Adams and others were also surveying our self-assured ascent to those peaks. And when they looked at the hard reality of the climb, they reached the conclusion that we didn't want to countenance – that armed struggle was not the route by which we could achieve our objectives. It is a credit to Adams's leadership that he set about winning the unwinnable war and brought a new, more pragmatic approach to republican politics.

Some have said that Adams and the republican leadership adopted a cynical approach to the crisis in order to begin the climb to those summits. These people believe that the leadership took the view that the strike should continue at least until Owen Carron, the republican candidate for Bobby Sands's vacant Fermanagh/South Tyrone seat, was elected.

At first, my natural republican instincts told me not to open up this potential can of worms, because, were it true, it would lay bare the most appalling vista: that the republican leadership sacrificed hunger strikers' lives.

This claim is founded on the Army Council's refusal to issue the order to end the hunger strike when it was patently clear that the five demands were not going to be granted. Bik McFarlane, the ultimate authority in the prison, leaves no room for doubt that, had the order to end the hunger strike been given, he would unquestionably have obeyed it. His 28 July comm clearly illustrated that at least half of the hunger strikers recognised that it was futile to continue with the fast and would have welcomed its end.

The republican leadership's public assertion that we prisoners were hell-bent on settling for nothing less than the full five demands was misleading.

Despite Adams's assertion to us, when the second bout of negotiations with the Mountain Climber broke down, that no damage would be done to the republican movement if we decided to end the hunger strike, the reality is different. If the hunger strike had ended before Carron faced the electorate in Fermanagh/South Tyrone, he would have lost the election: the broad nationalist electorate had allowed the republican movement to 'borrow' the seat to save Bobby's life, but it was never meant to be an unsecured loan. If no hunger strikers' lives were affected by the election, SDLP supporters would have called the loan in by refusing to put their 'X' beside a candidate who supported the armed struggle. After all, we need to remember that Bobby beat the unionist candidate, Harry West, by only 1,446 votes.

To put all this in perspective, we must bear in mind that the republican movement endorsed the 'ballot box and Armalite' strategy weeks after the hunger strike ended, at its November 1981 *ard fheis*. The fact that there was a sitting MP on the podium gave this monumental departure great credibility. (As we soon found out, Armalites do not fit into ballot boxes.)

Had Owen Carron not won that seat, the natural republican antagonism towards electoral politics would undoubtedly have asserted itself and thwarted the move into constitutional politics – and we could still be in a war situation today. Had Carron not set the ball rolling, hundreds, possibly a thousand, people who are alive today could be dead.

I tried, time and again, to search for a counter-balancing argument to the charge that the republican leadership let hunger strikers die to get Carron elected, because the conclusions to which I was being drawn frightened the life out of me. I told myself that Adams had informed the hunger strikers at the meeting in the camp hospital that there would be no damage to the republican movement if they decided to come off their fast (even though he must have known that the consequences of them immediately ending the hunger strike would have been catastrophic), and he had bluntly pointed out to them that there was every possibility that they all would die, and still not get their demands.

This approach would, on face value, have given the impression that Adams, speaking on behalf of the Army Council, wanted the remaining hunger strikers to end their fast voluntarily. I desperately wanted to believe that this was true. I was confounded by the fact that Pat Beag had been gagged, however. Perhaps one implication of this censorship is that the meeting was a charade – a media-driven, stage-managed act which would, in all probability, have only one outcome: the continuation of the hunger strike.

But why, I asked myself, would the 1981 IRA Army Council, if it wanted the hunger strike to continue, endanger the future direction of the entire struggle by allowing Adams to visit the hunger strikers at all, when the leadership knew from Bik's comm that several of them had questioned the wisdom of continuing the fast. Why take the risk? First, it would have been callous and damaging for the leadership not to have allowed Adams to go into the prison to explain the situation after he had been approached by the families to do so. The charge that the movement was manipulating the hunger strikers would have been immeasurably strengthened had their request been rejected. Second, there was the Lynch family's threat to call publicly for an end to the hunger strike, as outlined in Bik's comm which Adams received on 29 July – the day he visited the hunger strikers in the camp hospital. Was this a case of placating the Lynches and going for the lesser of the two evils? Perhaps, but that still didn't guarantee the Army Council that those hunger strikers who had questioned Bik the previous night about the tactics and the reasoning for continuing with the hunger strike wouldn't bring their defeatist attitude to the table and force an end to the hunger strike.

In the end, I reluctantly concluded that there was a case for the Army Council to answer. That is not to say that I am indicting them, but there are serious questions that have not been answered to date. Perhaps their actions can be justified.

I take no pleasure in criticising the 1981 IRA Army Council; in fact it strikes against every tenet of republicanism I have cherished throughout my life. Yet there can be no doubt that the Army Council called the shots during the hunger strike. The rank and file members of the IRA regard the Army Council as the only legitimate government in Ireland and when they offer 'advice', they don't intend it to be meant as friendly counsel from an agony aunt, but as a statement of their wishes. The Army Council knew its 'advice' would be taken, just as Bik and I knew we would be tempting fate by ignoring it. Arguably, it was submission to such rigid discipline that helped to produce the disaster that the second hunger strike became. Nor do I make any apology for saying that the Army Council acted in an inexcusable manner. The refusal of Council members, and their representatives, to bear *any* responsibility for what happened during the hunger strike is offensive.

To fellow republicans, I say: ten comrades died here. Not just my comrades, but *all* our comrades. We were *all* brothers, whether we came from the mountains of Pomeroy, the shores of Lough Neagh, the farmyards of Crossmaglen, the lakes of Fermanagh, the fishing villages of County Down or the back streets of Belfast and Derry. We all lived – and some of us died – for the Republic. I make no apology for the fact that this narrative challenges every one of us and forces us to confront unsavoury truths. While facing unsavoury truths was never our strong point, there comes a time when we must honestly face the murkier side of our past and admit that sometimes we were wrong. If ever there were such a need, the 1981 hunger strike is it.

In 1985, two years after my release from jail, I had an opportunity to see all the comms that had been written to the Army Council from the start of the protest. I got to read them because David Beresford was researching his seminal book *Ten Men Dead*, and I had been asked by the leadership to vet the comms that Beresford was receiving from the republican movement. Two other republicans, neither of whom had been involved in the prison struggle, were designated to assist me. Our instructions were to remove every reference to the Mountain Climber, so that Beresford would remain ignorant both about the existence of this person and the role he had played in the prison protest. But, unbeknownst to me, one of the other men must have let a comm slip through the net. After the process was completed, Beresford and I met in his Malone Road flat over a cup of coffee, ostensibly to clear up some trivial queries. We chatted for a while about this and that, and then suddenly he looked me in the eye and bluntly asked me: 'Who's the Mountain Climber, Ricky?' I was stunned and visibly unprepared for his question – a reaction that must have confirmed to him that he had stumbled on to something big. My mumbled response only compounded the problem, and I suggested, on the spur of the moment, that he should talk to Gerry Adams, who might, or might not, give him an answer. Beresford's account of the hunger strike suggests that whoever it was he spoke to confirmed the Mountain Climber's existence, but it was a carefully controlled confirmation. Once the cat was out of the bag, the damage-limitation exercise came into play.

While working with Beresford, I read dozens of comms that had been sent out of the jail during those terrible months of 1981, but I did not read all those addressed to the Army Council. One was missing: the fateful comm from Bik accepting the Mountain Climber deal had disappeared from the archives, its fate unknown, but its absence surely significant.

Years later, I had a discussion with Danny Morrison and Jim Gibney about a book that Danny was writing in relation to the H-Blocks, and I suggested to Danny that if he was going to write at all, he should 'Write the truth.' When Danny asked me what I meant by that remark, I assumed that he knew about the fact that the prison leadership had accepted the Mountain Climber deal that he had told Bik about when he visited the prison on 5 July 1981. To my astonishment, his mouth dropped open in surprise. Both men were members of the 'committee' (along with Gerry Adams and Liam Óg) which discussed the strategy of the hunger strike; yet both convinced me they knew nothing of our acceptance of the Mountain Climber deal. I found that amazing. Clearly Danny Morrison and Jim Gibney had been excluded from the circle of knowledge. But other members of the 'committee' did know about the missing comm and the Army Council's rejection of the Mountain Climber's deal, although that circle of knowledge, as I discovered, was very small indeed.

In 1991, I had a discussion about all this with a leading republican, a man who remained in the background but who was privy to all the intricacies of the hunger strike. I told him that I was very angry and upset about the manner in which the IRA leadership had handled the hunger strike, particularly the Army Council's rejection of our acceptance of the Mountain Climber deal. His reaction was revealing and damning. I would be wise, he told me, to stay silent about those events and that I 'could be shot' for speaking my thoughts in public. I heeded the warning, and once again let down the hunger strikers.

My own conscience and personal reservations aside, I also had to consider the effect that this narrative would have on the families of the dead hunger strikers. I had to ask myself if I should let sleeping dogs lie for their sakes – as well as for my own. I agonised over whether or not the families really wanted to hear what I had to say. I couldn't answer that question.

But there was something else: a persuasive voice, which refused to be silent, whispered that I had no right to paper over the truth or to deny the families and the Irish people my first-hand account of what had happened. I became convinced that the dead hunger strikers, denied any voice, would be dishonoured if I continued to silence my own. Justice demands that the facts be told without prejudice or favour and not submerged in half-truths, which are also half-lies. The nagging voice prevailed. My sincere belief is that, in publishing this book, as Bobby Sands said in his poem 'The Rhythm of Time', 'I'm right.'

To the families of the departed hunger strikers, I ask for understanding of my part in the hunger strike. I acknowledge that I should have been stronger for the sake of your husbands and sons. With the release of the 4 July 1981 statement, and our acceptance of the Mountain Climber's proposals, Bik and I tried to end it before Joe McDonnell died, but we were unsuccessful. With the benefit of hindsight and with no small measure of regret, I now know that I should have called for an end to the strike sooner than I did. My own silence was reprehensible.

I ask the families of the dead hunger strikers to understand why I have written this book. Not only does it cast some light on a critical part of our lives, but I believe that you had a right to know the facts as I knew them. I also believe that the story of your loved ones should be fully and honestly told – free of all political concerns. Your loved ones were more than faces on a gable wall to me; they were my dear friends and valued comrades. Futhermore, my children, your children and future generations of Irish people have a right to the truth; history will judge us very harshly if we skim over such a momentous event, as we have up to now.

I still look forward to the day when the people of Ireland will see 'The Rising of the Moon' and enjoy the fruits of a thirty-two-county Republic, free from foreign interference. In that oft-quoted phrase that began its life in the dark, dank cells of the H-Blocks so many years ago: '*Tiocfaidh ár lá.*'

BIBLIOGRAPHY

Adams, Gerry. *Falls Memories*. Dingle, County Kerry: Brandon, 1982.

— , *The Politics of Irish Freedom*. Dingle, County Kerry: Brandon, 1986.

— , *Before the Dawn*. Dingle, County Kerry: Brandon, 1997.

— , *A Pathway to Peace*. Cork: Mercier Press, 1998.

Beresford, David. *Ten Men Dead*. London: Grafton Books, 1987.

Bishop, Patrick, and Eamonn Mallie. *The Provisional IRA*. London: Heinemann, 1987.

Campbell, Brian, Laurence McKeown and Felim O'Hagan. *Nor Meekly Serve My Time*. Belfast: Beyond the Pale Publications, 1994.

Clarke, Liam. *Broadening the Battlefield*. Dublin: Gill & Macmillan, 1987.

De Baroid, Ciaran. *Ballymurphy and the Irish War*. London: Pluto Press, 1989.

Faul, Father Denis. *The British Army and Special Branch Brutality*.

— , *The Black and Blue Book: Violations of Human Rights in Northern Ireland, 1968–1978*.

— , *The Castlereagh File: Allegations of RUC Brutality, 1976–1977.*

Feeney, Brian, David McKittrick, Seamus Kelters and Chris Thornton. *Lost Lives.* Edinburgh: Mainstream Publishing Company Ltd, 1999.

Moloney, Ed. *A Secret History of the IRA.* London: Allen Lane, The Penguin Press, 2003.

O'Malley, Padraig. *Biting at the Grave.* Boston, Massachusetts: Beacon Press, 1990.

Sands, Bobby. *The Diary of Bobby Sands.* Dublin: Sinn Féin Publicity Department, 1981.

— , *Prison Poems.* Dublin: Sinn Féin Publicity Department, 1981.

Taylor, Peter. *Provos.* London: Bloomsbury, 1997.

Uris, Leon. *Trinity.* New York: Doubleday, 1976.